World Religions
and
Human Liberation

FAITH MEETS FAITH
An Orbis Series in Interreligious Dialogue
Paul F. Knitter, General Editor

In our contemporary world, the many religions and spiritualities stand in need of greater intercommunication and cooperation. More than ever before, they must speak to, learn from, and work with each other, in order to maintain their own identity and vitality and so to contribute to fashioning a better world.

FAITH MEETS FAITH seeks to promote interreligious dialogue by providing an open forum for the exchanges between and among followers of different religious paths. While the series wants to encourage creative and bold responses to the new questions of pluralism confronting religious persons today, it also recognizes the present plurality of perspectives concerning the methods and content of interreligious dialogue.

This series, therefore, does not want to endorse any one school of thought. By making available to both the scholarly community and the general public works that represent a variety of religious and methodological viewpoints, FAITH MEETS FAITH hopes to foster and focus the emerging encounter among the religions of the world.

Already published:

FAITH MEETS FAITH SERIES

World Religions
and
Human Liberation

Edited by
Dan Cohn-Sherbok

ORBIS BOOKS

Maryknoll, New York 10545

The Catholic Foreign Mission Society of America (Maryknoll) recruits and trains people for overseas missionary service. Through Orbis Books, Maryknoll aims to foster the international dialogue that is essential to mission. The books published, however, reflect the opinions of their authors and are not meant to represent the official position of the Society.

Library of Congress Cataloging-in-Publication Data

World religions and human liberation / edited by Dan Cohn-Sherbok.
    p.   cm. — (Faith meets faith)
   Includes bibliographical references.
   ISBN 0-88344-796-7   ISBN 0-88344-795-9 (pbk.)
   1. Liberation theology.   2. Religions.   I. Cohn-Sherbok. Dan.
II. Series.
BT83.57.W67   1991
291.2 — dc20   91-47696
                                          CIP

Contents

Preface

DAN COHN-SHERBOK

Since the mid-1960s, liberation theology has been one of the most important theological developments worldwide. It has provoked controversy and confusion. It has also challenged a wide range of thinkers in Latin America, Africa, and Asia. Yet, despite the impact of this movement, liberation theology has evoked little formal response from the world religions. With few exceptions, thinkers in the major religions of the world have had little to say about the views of liberationists. The purpose of this collection of essays is to focus attention on the possible interconnections and discontinuities between Christian liberation theology and several of the world religions. It is the hope of all who have contributed to this dialogue that their reflection will highlight the significance of this new theological development in a global context.

The contributions come from scholars of Judaism, Christianity, Islam, Buddhism, Hinduism, and African traditional religions. Other faiths, of course, merit inclusion, but because of the limits of size and scope, it was felt necessary to limit this preliminary exploration to what are generally considered the best known world religions. We hope that this investigation will serve as a starting point for further reflections by representatives of such traditions. If so, it will have served its purposes, and our modest efforts will be amply rewarded.

Contributors were asked to base their reflections on two books: Gustavo Gutiérrez, *A Theology of Liberation* (Maryknoll, N.Y.: Orbis Books, 15th Anniversary edition, 1988), and Leonardo and Clodovis Boff, *Introducing Liberation Theology* (Orbis, 1987). In addition, they were asked to consider a set of key questions relating fundamental themes in liberation theology to their own traditions concerning: similarities and differences; possibilities of cooperation in the liberation venture; necessity of liberationist praxis for interpreting the religious tradition in question; the question of individual and social sin; relative importance of individual conversion or enlightenment in relation to removing evil social structures; violence and liberation; contribution of liberation theology to the author's tradition; and the contribution of that tradition to liberation theology.

For the sake of those who will not have had the opportunity to read the

Latin America and Beyond (New York: Pantheon Books, 1987), Phillip Berryman devotes only one out of thirteen chapters to the "beyond." There is no doubt that Latin America became a primary breeding ground for liberation theology in the years following Vatican II. After all, more than six hundred bishops from Latin America had attended the Second Vatican Council and had returned to their home countries to put into action the mandate of the Council to seek to eliminate the glaring social inequalities so pervasive in their own bailiwicks. They convened their own General Conference in Medellin, Colombia, in 1968; and from that Conference came the rallying cry which has become the *raison d'être* for liberation theology: the need to show "a preferential option for the poor." The Medellin Conference has been hailed as "the Vatican II of Latin America" and "the birthplace of liberation theology."

Certainly, many of the giants among third-world liberation theologians are Latin Americans. Gustavo Gutiérrez of Peru is considered preeminent, and his book *A Theology of Liberation* (English translation 1973) the original text for liberation theology. Leonardo Boff of Brazil has been a prime leader in articulating a new christology and ecclesiology in tune with liberation theology. Boff's *Church: Charism and Power: Liberation and the Institutional Church* (New York: Crossroad, 1985) expands upon the Vatican II notion of the church as "the people of God." His espousal of the base Christian communities of Latin America as the model of the Catholic church of the future, together with his charge that the present hierarchical model has been a seedbed for corruption, led to his recent year-long censure by papal authorities. In addition to Gutiérrez and Boff, one cannot even begin to appreciate the rich insights of liberation theology without giving serious attention to Juan Luis Segundo of Uruguay, Hugo Assmann of Brazil, José Porfirio Miranda and Enrique Dussel of Mexico, José Míguez Bonino of Argentina, Jon Sobrino and Elsa Tamez of San Salvador and many other Latin Americans.

Nevertheless, it would be a serious mistake, and a mistake often made by supporters and detractors alike, to consider third-world liberation theology primarily a Latin American phenomenon. This claim is not only false, but is correctly interpreted by non-Westerners as one more example of Western imperialism. African and Asian liberation theologians have made *equally important* contributions to the development of liberation theology. *African and Asian liberation theologies are not stepchildren of Latin American liberation theology.* They began to emerge in the 1960s at the same time and for the same reasons as Latin American liberation theology. African and Asian liberation theologies grew out of the involvement of these theologians in the lives of the poor and the influence of Vatican II upon their bishops and priests.

For example, Carlos Abesamis of the Philippines maintains that during the summers he spent working as a priest in the rural areas surrounding Manila in the late 1960s and early 1970s, he became immersed in the experience of the poor, which, in turn, led him to see biblical teachings from a third-world perspective. Tissa Balasuriya of Sri Lanka recalls discussions he had with Gustavo Gutiérrez in 1968 at a conference in Geneva sponsored by the World Council of Churches. According to Balasuriya, these discussions, which focused upon their common concerns for the poor in their respective countries, contained the seeds of liberation theology. So it is understandable that Africans and Asians are sensitive to the common misperception that their role in the development of liberation theology was minimal. Engelbert Mveng of Cameroun maintains that the Ecumenical Association of Third World Theologians (EATWOT), established in 1976, was an African inspiration that took root in Louvain in the mid-1970s among young African theologians. Even subsequent to that meeting in 1976, Mveng laments that many of their Latin American counterparts still did not take African and Asian theologians seriously. Little wonder that African and Asian theologians believe that third-world theologies must be de-westernized as well as decolonialized.

It is quite clear that the distinctive features of African and Asian liberation theologies present important challenges to world religions. A special ingredient of African liberation theology that sets it apart from its Latin American counterpart is its focus upon the problem of indigenization and the role of native African religions. A unique dimension of Asian liberation theology is its setting within a plurality of religious faiths. In Asia, Christianity is but a small religious minority. Indigenization and religious pluralism are important challenges, not only to the Christian faith, but to the other world religions as well.

Given the very different religious milieus in which liberation theologies continue to emerge and develop, the immense diversity within liberation theology throughout the continents of Africa, Asia, and Latin America is not surprising. Liberation theologies defy simple schemes of classification. *Liberation theology is by no means a monolithic movement.* For the purpose of this essay I shall focus upon eight features of liberation theology that could have important ramifications for the religions of the world.

A PREFERENTIAL OPTION FOR THE POOR

Christian liberation theology stands foursquare in the Jewish prophetic tradition in showing "a preferential option for the poor." A typical model for this affirmation is the prophet Amos who, after blaming Israel's neighbors for their immoral behavior and lack of concern for their needy, saved his severest condemnation for Israel herself—for her people selling "the righteous for silver, and the needy for a pair of shoes" (Amos 2:6). This overriding concern for the plight of the poor, the needy, and the afflicted, so deeply imbedded in the Jewish prophetic tradition, is the linchpin of Christian liberation theology. All other convictions emerge from this fundamental affirmation.

God becomes the Great Liberator who sides with the oppressed, a theme exemplified in the Exodus story of the liberation of the Jewish people from the chains of their Egyptian oppressors. Christian liberation theologians link this exodus theme with the resurrection event, making the latter a kind of sequel to the exodus, a latter stage in God's plan for liberation. Christian liberation theologians note that Jesus expressed his concern for the oppressed in his very first sermon: "The Spirit of the Lord is upon me, because he has anointed me to preach good news to the poor. He has sent me to proclaim release to the captives and recovering of sight to the blind, to set at liberty those who are oppressed" (Luke 4:18). The ethical teachings of Jesus reflect a fundamental concern for the poor with deep roots in the Jewish prophetic tradition. The well-known story of the Good Samaritan suggests that caring for the one left helpless by the side of the road is the essence of true religion. The Beatitudes reflect this same theme: "Blessed are the poor in spirit, for theirs is the kingdom of heaven. Blessed are those who mourn, for they shall be comforted. Blessed are the meek, for they shall inherit the earth." And "blessed are those who are persecuted for righteousness' sake, for theirs is the kingdom of heaven" (Matt. 5). So when Jesus points out those whom God favors and who will inherit the kingdom, he singles out the hungry, the thirsty, the stranger, the naked, and the sick. And he makes clear to his followers that their commitment to him is best expressed in their preferential concern for the needy: "Truly, I say to you, as you did it not to one of the least of these, you did it not to me" (Matt. 25:45). We shall note later how this focus on the ethical teachings of Jesus implies a distinctive christology for liberation theologians.

A preferential option for the poor does not necessarily mean an exclusive concern for the poor at the expense of the well-to-do. God loves all people and wants to liberate all people from situations that render them less than human. Nevertheless, the poor and oppressed deserve special treatment, because they lack the power to have complete control over their destiny. The wealthy are reluctant to give up their privileged position, although they have the power to do so. Because they refuse to exercise this power, Jesus tells his disciples that "it is easier for a camel to go through the eye of a needle than for a rich man to enter the kingdom of God" (Matt. 19:24). Since the rich exercise their power to keep the poor powerless, the poor need God's special concern to assist them in achieving liberation. After all, they constitute the vast majority of people in this world, and their numbers continue to increase, prompting liberation theologians to speak of "the irruption of the poor."

When, therefore, the Second Vatican Council in the early 1960s urged the nations of the world to "remove the immense economic inequalities," and stressed that the joys and hopes of this age must be directed especially to "those who are poor or in any way afflicted," liberation theologians accepted this mandate as their number-one God-given call. And when the Medellin Conference of Latin American bishops urged their people to "defend the rights of the poor and oppressed according to the gospel commandment," liberation theologians again accepted the challenge. It is essential to stress the fact that liberation theologians center this "preferential option for the poor" in the gospel. This same point is made forcefully by Archbishop Desmond Tutu of South Africa, who insists that the reason why apartheid must be considered "evil, totally and without remainder" is that "the Christian Bible and the gospel of Jesus Christ our Lord is subversive of all injustice and evil, oppression and exploitation, and that God is on the side of the oppressed and downtrodden."[1]

God's "preferential option for the poor" unites the Jewish prophetic tradition with Christian liberation theology. Here Dan Cohn-Sherbok sees a crucial challenge for both Jew and Christian: "The Jesus of the New Testament can be understood as Jesus the Jew, who, like the great prophets of ancient Israel, struggled to rescue the nation from its iniquity and to draw the people back to the faith of their ancestors. The theologians of liberation present the Christian faith as being a further manifestation of the living tradition of social concern and idealism which has animated traditional Judaism through the centuries. Here, then, in the life of Jesus as interpreted by liberation theologians, is a link that can draw Jews and Christians together in a mutual quest for the elimination of oppression and injustice in the modern world."[2] Can this "preferential option for the poor" also be a link between Judaism and Christianity and the other major religions of the world?

BASE CHRISTIAN (HUMAN) COMMUNITIES

If the preferential option for the poor is the basic theme of liberation theology, one of its corollaries is that theology should emerge from the poor people themselves, from the small communities of the oppressed who forge their own beliefs on the basis of their collective experience. This approach is called "a people's version of theology."

Traditionally Christian theology has been a "theology from above." This approach has been especially evident in the Roman Catholic church, in which the pope or church council decides the proper teachings of the church and in hierarchical fashion passes these teachings down through the proper authorities, bishops to priests to laity, from the top to the bottom. The responsibility of the people on the bottom, the lay people, is to "pray, pay and obey." Even for priests, obedience has been the primary virtue. As one American priest said of his seminary training of the 1950s, "For eight years, they dressed you like a girl and treated you like a child. And then they expected you to be a man." He added that lay people in turn were expected to be obedient to the priest: "Nobody criticized you. It was wonderful. We had all the answers. And the parishioners didn't even know what questions to ask. If they didn't go along with you, you simply said they were going to Hell. I condemned more people to Hell than I care to remember."[3]

Liberation theology reverses this top-to-bottom process. Theology arises from the grassroots, from small groups of lay people who come together to pray, to study Scripture, to reflect, and to relate their faith to their everyday lives. This is "theology from below." The members of these small groups ask themselves: What does it mean when Jesus says to us, "I have come that you may have life and have it with abundance," or "I have come to set you at liberty," or "Blessed are the poor in spirit, for theirs is the kingdom of heaven"? Liberation theology does not begin with popes or councils or clergy or even professional theologians. Rather, it emerges from "the underside of history" and moves upward to the theologians of liberation who perform "the second act" of theology, that is, articulating a "feet-on-the-ground" theology of the poor people themselves.

Liberation theology has no individual founders or high priests. The base Christian communities (CEBs) are its source and lifeblood. During the past two decades, base Christian communities have sprouted up throughout the Third World. It is estimated that in the early 1980s, in the country of Brazil alone, over eighty thousand such communities were thriving. How can we describe these communities? In his book *Basic Ecclesial Communities: The Evangelization of the Poor*, Alvaro Barriero answers:

> They are places of communion, where the presence of the Kingdom of God, which is a kingdom of justice, peace, and love, is manifested sacramentally, that is, visibly and effectively. They are communities of poor people who are living and trying to live increasingly, faith, hope, and love. This incarnation is as simple as it is radical, and as fragile as it is transforming. It is in the nature of the incarnation of the Word in the flesh of humankind.[4]

Given this approach to theology, one can understand liberation theologian Pablo Richard's comment that the poor have taught him everything. For, in a very real sense, these communities are the teachers, the theologians are the students.

This radically different view of theology coming from below presents a serious challenge to the traditional view both of theology and of the nature of the church. In Barriero's words, it raises two crucial questions: "1. Can the poor be the evangelizers and liberators of their oppressors? 2. How can the poor in the CEBs evangelize and liberate the very church from which they received the gospel of liberation?"[5] It is no surprise, then, that the established churches today consider liberation theology and the base Christian communities a serious threat.

The continent of Asia presents its own distinctive challenge in this new theological approach. In Latin America with its overwhelming Christian—particularly Roman Catholic—constituency, these small communities are exclusively Christian. But in Asia, where Christians constitute but 3 per cent of the population, these small groups become in many areas base *human* communities that include participants from different religious backgrounds who share their common concerns. In Sri Lanka, for example, Aloysius Pieris, a Roman Catholic priest who has spent his professional life studying Buddhism and immersing himself in Buddhist communal life, has become convinced that "liberation theology begins to be formulated only when a given Christian community begins to be drawn into the local peoples' struggle for full humanity and through that struggle begins to sink its roots in the lives and cultures of these people, most of whom, in our continent, happen to be non-Christian."[6] Pieris urges "complementary cooperation," with Buddhists and Christians coming together in base human communities in their common struggle against poverty and oppression.

Here, then, is another critical challenge for world faiths. Can these different religions encourage the formation of base human communities from "the underside of history" who will struggle as one family against their common oppressors?

THE CHALLENGE OF INDIGENIZATION

Since base communities of the poor and oppressed differ radically across the Third World in terms of their culture, customs, and language, it is obvious that the medium in which the message of Christianity is delivered must not only be liberated from first-world versions, but must also be translated into a large variety of forms reflecting each local situation. Christianity can only make sense in terms of what the local people can understand and assimilate into their own consciousness. As African theologian Edward Fashole-Luke maintains, theologians must theologize primarily for their own local communities. Here, then, is the problem of indigenization, or what is often called the need for cultural liberation. The problem can be stated in this fashion: To what degree can the Christian faith be translated into local cultural patterns, practices, and beliefs without losing the core of the faith itself? Heretofore, it had been assumed by many interpreters of Christianity that the Western classical version of the faith was couched in a universal package that was valid for all areas of the world. But liberation theologians are among those who insist that the challenge of indigenization must be taken seriously. It is better to err on the side of full authentic indigenization — a local people's version of theology — than to permit Christianity to claim a universal form which is largely a Western import.

As a vivid example of indigenization, let us consider Kosuke Koyama's book *Waterbuffalo Theology*. Here Koyama translates his understanding of the Christian faith into language and concepts native to the people of Thailand, language and concepts so different from Western versions. In forging a Thailand theology "from below," Koyama insists that "it is wrong to say that we must produce an indigenous theology. It is not necessary to produce one. It is there!"[7] A theology coming out of people who spend their waking hours with waterbuffaloes in the rice fields finds expression in such terminology as "leaking house," "bicycle," "rainy season," "sticky-rice," "cock-fighting," and so on.[8] Koyama adds: "God has called me to work here in northern Thailand, not in Italy or Switzerland. And I am working with neither a Thomas Aquinas nor a Karl Barth. God commanded me to be a neighbor to these farmers."[9]

Obviously, the situation in Thailand differs not only from the First World, but also from other localities in the Third World. Theology cannot be transported lock, stock, and barrel from Thailand to Peru or Kenya any more than it can from Rome to Korea. Take Africa as another example. On this continent, increasing attention has been directed in the past two decades to native religions and how they can be incorporated into Christian theology. How does African culture — or, rather, cultures — shape the Christian message? Heretofore, native African religions have been considered pagan by most Western Christian missionaries. Converts to Christianity were expected to renounce their native religious practices. Indeed, the rapid growth of independent Christian churches in Africa has been due largely to their effort to take native religions seriously, so unlike the established churches and their dependence on Western forms. Gwinyai H. Muzorewa states the newer approach: "I believe that indigenized Christianity will be able to transform a people without condemning their cultural identity. The African independent churches, which consciously promote religious practices affirming African humanity, are in a position to accomplish this transformation."[10]

To be sure, the promotion of "religious practices affirming African humanity" can be a controversial issue. Take, for example, the practice of polygamy, so deeply imbedded in many African cultures, a practice that conflicts head-on with the Western Christian norm of monogamy. Must this Western norm be accepted by African Christians? If an African man with several wives converts to Christianity, which wives should he kick out of his home — if any? Or might there be a "grandfather clause" that protects converts? If the Western ideal of monogamy becomes *the* norm for Africans, is this not one more example of a Western ideal being imposed on a non-Western culture that accepts polygamy as morally legitimate? In his book *Polygamy Reconsidered*, Eugene Hillman insists:

> The traditional ecclesiastical discipline regarding African polygamy is not as well founded, biblically and theologically, as has been supposed heretofore ... Since the available evidence indicates, moreover, that this form of plural marriage still sustains important social values in most African societies and that it will continue to be practiced widely among African peoples in the foreseeable future, it would be morally irresponsible for Church leaders and theologians to simply ignore the

missionary and pastoral implications of such a problematic discipline.[11]

Most liberation theologians would agree with Hillman. They would also cite ancestor worship and spiritual healing through the agency of witch doctors as other practices worth incorporating into the Christian heritage.

Another important example of indigenization in the Third World is Korean Minjung theology, which incorporates elements from Korean native religion. Koreans understandably want to shed their Western Christian excess baggage and reaffirm the cultural integrity of their own religious heritage. *Minjung* refers to the oppressed and exploited in Korean society who seek liberation and justice in the context of their own distinctive shamanistic culture. Here we have a cultural world populated by a myriad of spiritual beings which literally permeate the everyday lives of the ordinary people, a kind of polytheism that meets resistance from the Western Christian norm of radical monotheism. Does Minjung theology constitute a threat or a positive response for Korean Christianity? The religious beliefs and practices of individuals and societies betray an incredible multiplicity of phenomena throughout the Third World. Indigenization is a challenge to all world religions. How does one separate the extraneous from the essential, the chaff from the wheat? The challenge for every world religion is not only to make clear what their essentials are that cannot be compromised, but also to acknowledge the kinds of roadblocks these "essentials" set up in the contacts that these world religions have with one another. Can these roadblocks be removed in part, or at least modified in the process of indigenization?

A NEW METHODOLOGY

In his book *Waterbuffalo Theology*, Kosuke Koyama suggests two different approaches to theology: "living room" and "kitchen." The former is formal theology, the theological method of Western classical Christianity. It is the theology proclaimed by popes and church councils, written about in books and transmitted by ministers and missionaries. It is the method in which lay people sit in the living rooms with their hands folded, receiving the truths from the churches' official emissaries. On the other hand, "kitchen theology" is informal theology. It emerges from the everyday lives of the poor and oppressed as they squat on their dirt kitchen floors, praying and reflecting on their faith and practice. As Koyama expresses it:

I have discovered that the seasoning takes place in the Thai theological kitchen, not in the broad living room into which missionaries have access. Their theological activity goes on while they squat on the dirt ground, and not while sipping tea with missionary friends in the teak-floored shiny living room ... My experience in peeping into the kitchen is sometimes like watching a great Chinese chef throwing six different ingredients into a heated oil kwali.[12]

Western Christian theological method has been for the most part living-room oriented. But in liberation theology, the kitchen takes over and methodology is turned upside down. Here theological method is down-to-earth, fragmentary, incomplete, and pluralistic. Here we have the constant interplay of many different ingredients making up the Christian menu: Bible reading, prayer, discussion, reflection—flavored, as Koyama puts it, with "Aristotelian pepper and Buddhist salt."

Another way of expressing this new methodology is by means of the phrase "the hermeneutical circle," one used by many Latin American theologians of liberation. They warn against any theology or ideology which claims purity and universality, a warning which they term "ideological suspicion." Juan Luis Segundo of Uruguay sees four integrating factors essential to theological methodology or what he calls the "hermeneutical circle":

Firstly, there is our way of experiencing reality, which leads us to ideological suspicion. *Secondly*, there is the application of our ideological suspicion to the whole ideological superstructure in general and to theology in particular. *Thirdly*, there comes a new way of experiencing theological reality that leads us to exegetical suspicion, that is, to the suspicion that the prevailing interpretation of the Bible has not taken important pieces of data into account. *Fourthly*, we have our new hermeneutic, that is our new way of interpreting the fountainhead of our faith (i.e. Scripture) with the new elements at our disposal.[13]

This theological methodology which emphasizes continuing action and reflection is called *praxis*. In this methodology, action and involvement in the life of the world take precedence over reflection and interpretation, although the latter have their essential role. But reflection comes *after* action as a "second act." This theological method centered on praxis means that truth cannot be prepackaged nor ever be considered a final product; one must be "ideologically suspicious" about any such claim. Truth is in constant flux and continues to grow and change as the hermeneutical circle revolves. Praxis keeps life and faith together, not as a series of finished dogmas applicable for all times and places, but as a reflection of the "kitchen" experiences of the base communities. One might say that in a very real sense, "the medium is the message"—this method of doing theology incarnates the message itself.

Because the methodology of liberation theology places heavy emphasis on the everyday lives of the poor in their oppressive societies, the social sciences become an indispensable tool for understanding the causes of this oppression. And Marxist analysis which sees class struggle—the rich controlling the lives of the poor—as a prime cause of social oppression becomes crucial. In thus incorporating the insights of Marxist social analysis, liberation theologians are often branded Marxists by many of their critics. But if Marxism as a full-blown ideology denies God or Transcendence and thereby affirms the material here-and-now as the only reality, then one would be hard put to single out any liberation theologian today as Marxist. To utilize Marxist insights in ascertaining the root causes of human oppression does not make one a Marxist any more than to use Freudian insights in seeking to understand human behavior thereby makes one a Freudian.

Along this same line, it is fair to note that, in determining the root causes of social inequalities in the Third World, liberation theologians without hesitation point the finger of condemnation at the excesses of capitalism, in which the profit motive becomes so overwhelming that glaring social injustice results. But the condemnation of the excesses of capitalism does not put liberation theologians necessarily on the socialist bandwagon. What these theologians want is the kind of society which promotes liberation and justice, a society in which there is a much more equitable redistribution of wealth and resources than is presently to be found in most parts of the Third World. Here labels are not important; human dignity is.

The theological method of liberation theology is a distinct contrast to the classical Western Christian model. Its clarion call—begin with the everyday lives of the poor and oppressed!—also constitutes a challenge to other religions.

SIN AND EVIL AS BOTH PERSONAL AND SYSTEMIC

For liberation theologians, salvation is not primarily something to be achieved or awarded in a future life. Salvation essentially includes liberation from the evil and sins of this world, from poverty and oppression and all those ingredients which perpetuate inhumanity. In short, salvation and liberation are twin components; one has no meaning without the other. Overcoming sin and evil is the primary goal of salvation which in turn constitutes liberation.

For liberation theologians, evil is dehumanization. And sin is that demonic impulse within every individual to use one's own power to achieve one's own goals at the expense of the humanity of others. Sin or evil is manifested in two dimensions: personal and social. In the former, one's pride, one's obsession with self-interest degrades the divine image within the individual as well as one's relationships with others. In the latter, evil becomes institutionalized in a social system and must be eradicated by social means.

Personal sin has been the dominant emphasis in Western classical Christian theology. Here the Pauline model is stressed: "I do not understand my own actions, for I do not do what I want, but I do the very thing I hate . . . I can will what is right, but I cannot do it. For I do not do the good I want, but the evil I do not want is what I do" (Rom. 7:15, 18, 19). Liberation theologians are part of this Pauline tradition that affirms the depth and reality of personal sin. Critics often miss this point.

But liberation theologians differ from the classical position regarding sin and evil in insisting that sin and evil must be understood and addressed in the social dimension as well: what is termed *systemic* sin or evil. Each individual exists within social structures that themselves perpetuate injustice. Societies can be so constructed as to breed poverty, sexism, racism, and other dimensions of inhumanity. No matter how exemplary personal lives may be, a change of heart in people's personal lives will not of itself change the system. Systemic evil has its own causes and requires its own solutions.

Liberation theologians bear down hard on this point. They contend that systemic evil can be eliminated only if the social structures that perpetuate such evil are changed. It is not sufficient to reform individual lives, although that goal in itself is important. If, for example, a particular capitalist system breeds excess injustices, the system must be changed. If a particular socialist system inhibits personal incentive, the system must be changed. If any society perpetuates a caste system into which people are born and from which they cannot escape, the system must be changed.

In overcoming systemic evil, liberation theologians are skeptical of those who advocate reform gradually over a long period of time. Gradual reform more often than not means no genuine reform. In the early 1970s Gustavo Gutiérrez and many of his Latin American colleagues became impatient with what was called the *development* model of reform which contends that foreign countries can improve the living conditions of the poor by means of foreign economic investments. But such an approach leaves the unjust structures of the present system intact. In Gutiérrez's own words:

> The poor countries are becoming ever more clearly aware that their underdevelopment is only the by-product of the development of other countries . . . they are realizing that their own development will come about only with a struggle to break the domination of the rich countries. Only a radical break from the status quo, that is, a profound transformation of the private property system, access to power of the exploited class, and a social revolution that would break this dependence would allow for the change to a new society . . . only a break with the unjust order and a frank commitment to a new society can make the message of love which the Christian community bears credible to Latin Americans.[14]

Another important point that should be underscored here is what liberation theologians mean by *violence*. Violence is not only of the physical variety; violence in its wider meaning is dehumanization. Thus, when Gutiérrez writes of the need to "struggle to break the domination of the rich countries," to make "a radical break from the status quo," to advocate "a social revolution that would break this dependence," he is not naively suggesting that violence is about to be introduced into a nonviolent society. *Violence is already there, imbedded in an unjust society.* Violence is oppression, poverty, racism, sexism: anything that degrades human beings and keeps them from achieving their dignity. The problem for liberation theologians is how to eradicate this vicious systemic violence. To acquiesce in and thereby condone systemic violence is simply to perpetuate it.

Here again we should note that, although liberation theologians speak with one voice in condemning systemic violence and in dedicating themselves to its elimination, this writer knows of no liberation theologians who at the present time advocate *physical violence*. They would not survive if they did! The two prominent Latin American liberation theologians who did advocate violence, Che Guevara and Camilo Torres, represent a precedent and an illustration of what happens to theologians who advocate physical violence. Both were martyred for their convictions.

Where to draw the line in suggesting ways to overcome and eliminate an evil and violent social system is a painful and controversial problem. Consider Archbishop Desmond Tutu of South Africa. Tutu has been uncompromising in his verbal denunciation of the apartheid system as "positively unbiblical, un-Christian, immoral and evil." One cannot speak more clearly than that. He has even compared the present South African government that perpetuates apartheid to that of Nazi Germany. He has predicted that there will soon be a black prime minister in South Africa. And yet, to date he has refrained from advocating physical violence to overcome apartheid, because he knows that the oppressed do not have the power to use such means, even if under some circumstances he were to consider such means just. But this does not stop him from urging every other means short of physical violence to overcome the apartheid system. And here is the irony: the oppressor can use physical violence, the oppressed cannot. It would be difficult to imagine a more pernicious example of systemic evil than apartheid.

GOD AS LIBERATOR

"The central question in Latin America today is not atheism—the ontological question of whether or not God exists. The central issue is *idolatry*— a worship of the false gods of the system of oppression. Even more tragic than atheism is the faith and hope that is put in false gods. Much to the contrary of what might be supposed, false gods not only exist today, but are in excellent health!"[15]

This statement by a group of Latin American liberation theologians is one with which all liberation theologians would agree. These theologians contend that the poor and oppressed *know* that God exists. But they wonder whether God cares for them, whether God is with them in their struggle for liberation. To find the answer they turn to their Bibles. And here they discover that the Biblical notion of God is a reaffirmation of the Jewish prophetic tradition, namely, to know God is to do justice. Said the prophet Micah: "What does the Lord require of thee but to do justice?" This is God's nature.

In the Western Christian classical tradition the basic theological question has been the ontological one: Does God in fact exist? What are the arguments for God's existence? Hence, the ontological, cosmological, teleological, and moral arguments, so much a part of classical theology. And how has God's existence and nature been revealed through Christ and the church? In this approach, a dualism in the nature of reality has been assumed: God over against humanity, eternal over against temporal, transcendence over against immanence, even man over against woman, and spirit over against flesh. How can these gaps be bridged? How can humanity know God the Father, how can transcendence penetrate immanence? Since the divine was separate from the human realm, the problem was how the two intersected, how the divine became known to the human.

Liberation theology focuses on God's activity rather than God's existence. Liberation fuses the transcendent and the immanent. In this fusion the activity of God and the pursuit of justice become one and the same. As Bishop Casaldáliga puts it: "Where you say peace, justice, love, I say God! Where you say God, I say freedom, justice, love!"[16] The problem for liberation theologians is the opposite of that of classical theologians. For the latter, the problem has been how God and humanity intersect. For the former the problem is how they remain distinct.

In emphasizing idolatry as a key issue liberation theologians point out how the God of the oppressor supports the status quo. This God makes the rich feel comfortable in their oppressor state. For this reason, Hugo Assmann insists that "the god of the rich and the God of the poor are not the same God."[17] The God of the poor is the liberator God who brings hope to those who struggle for justice. The God of the poor is the God of the Jewish prophetic tradition, the God who saves God's people from the hands of the Egyptians, who leads them to a promised land, who comforts and succors them in times of tribulation. The God of the poor is the One who anointed Jesus "to preach good news to the poor, and to set at liberty those who are oppressed."

This conviction that God is the active force for justice and love has important implications for world religions. The traditional Western Christian view of God as separate and unique has often been a stumbling block in Christianity's relationship with other religions. But if God is justice and love in action on the side of the poor, this could have important parallels with other religions. As C. S. Song points out in *The Compassionate God*, surely "God must be capable of hearing, understanding, and responding to the cries of humanity uttered in different languages, the hopes and despair expressed in diverse cultural and religious symbols. Christian theology has barely begun to hear and understand these languages and symbols. Are these languages and symbols so different from our Christian language and symbols?" The core of the religious life, Song argues, is "the human spirit in agony and in hope," a spirit found in all religions. This human spirit, a reflection of the divine spirit, "does work in diverse and strange ways. That is why we as Christians must be alert if we want to see God's signals in the lives of other peoples, to understand God's signs in the history of other nations, and to decipher God's will in the struggle of suffering persons outside the familiar domain of Christianity."[18]

Tissa Balasuriya of Sri Lanka suggests the need for a *planetary theology*, one that transcends particular ideologies and religions, one whose goal is to arrive at "a higher, wider and deeper level of sharing among all human beings."[19] Here Song's compassionate God becomes the central focus, this compassion for justice which is the only hope for humanity, both for "the poor and the rich, the oppressed and the oppressors, the theists and the atheists, Christians, Muslims, Jews, Buddhists and Hindus. Until the time when the communion of love is firmly established in the world of strife and conflict, of pain and suffering, God moves on in compassion. We have no alternative but to move on with God toward that vision of a community of compassion and communion of love."[20] Can the conviction of God as Liberator be an important avenue for cooperation among world religions?

CHRIST AS LIBERATOR OF THE HUMAN CONDITION

"Without the preaching of justice there is no Gospel of Jesus Christ. This is not to politicize the Church; it is to be faithful. And if we are not faithful, we mutilate the heart of Jesus' message and we pervert the very mission of the Church."[21] Here Leonardo Boff underscores the basic tenet of christology for most liberation theologians: justice and the gospel of Jesus Christ are inseparable. One is not possible without the other.

Leonardo Boff and other liberation theologians contend that in the history of Christian theology there have been two distinctly different christologies competing for the allegiance of theologians: "christology from above" and "christology from below." The former, which has been the dominant Western classical view, has stressed Jesus' divinity, that Jesus is God who became human, the divine incarnate in the human. Here one begins with the proclamation that Jesus is one with God, that in Jesus God *descends* to the level of humanity. The uniqueness and transcendence and revealed divine nature of Christ take precedence over his immanence and humanity. That is "christology from above." On the other hand, a "christology from below"—and here Boff points to St. Francis as the model—begins with Jesus as a fully human being who in and through his humanity reveals his divinity. Jesus' identification with his fellow human beings and particularly with the poor and oppressed is the starting point for christology. Through his humanity, Jesus *ascends* to his divinity, to his Godliness.

Most liberation theologians take their stand with the "christology from below" approach, insisting that this view of Jesus is more compatible with his ministry of bringing the Good News to the poor and setting at liberty those who are oppressed in expressing the humanity of Jesus. Leonardo Boff describes Jesus with such phrases as the liberator of the human condition; a person of extraordinary good sense, creative imagination and originality; a human being with complete openness to God and humanity; one who practices indiscriminate love without limits: in short, *the human being par excellence*. For Boff, the resurrection of Jesus affirms Jesus' humanity as the central key to liberation. It is the affirmation that his humanity ascends to his divinity. The responsibility of the followers of Jesus is to express this resurrected Jesus in their daily lives. In Boff's words: "Wherever people seek the good, justice, humanitarian love, solidarity, communion, and understanding between people, wherever they dedicate themselves to overcoming their own egoism, making this world more human and fraternal, and opening themselves to the normative Transcendent for their lives, there we can say, with all certainty that the resurrected one is present, because the cause for which he lived, suffered, was tried and executed is being carried forward."[22]

The "christology from below" approach has important implications for the relationship between Christianity and other world religions. Jesus' identification with the Jewish prophetic tradition has already been mentioned. Jesus himself claims that he came to fulfill the Jewish law and the prophets. By this he meant the continuing affirmation of the ethical dimension of faith: that God as justice and love is on the side of the poor in their struggle for human liberation.

In Asia, with its plurality of religions, liberation theologians believe that the "christology from below" approach is necessary if the message of Jesus is to have a significant impact on the Asian people. This approach can build bridges between Jesus and the prophets of Eastern religions. For example, Aloysius Pieris points to a Buddhism of *ascent* and *descent*. Like their Christian counterparts, the first emphasizes the Buddha as a human being who eventually arrives at the state of mind known as *nirvana*. The latter begins with the Buddha's identification with the eternal *dharma* who descends into a human incarnation. By opting for the *ascent* approach in both Buddhism and Christianity, Pieris argues that "an Asian theology of liberation evolves into a christology that does not compete with but complements buddhology by acknowledging the one path of liberation on which Christians join Buddhists in their gnostic detachment (or the practice of voluntary poverty) and Buddhists join Christians' agapeic involvement in the struggle against involuntary poverty."[23]

In like manner, Kosuke Koyama objects to the traditional approach of the Western missionary who affirmed the uniqueness and superiority of Christ. Asians show no interest in that kind of christology. Koyama defines the proper role of the missionary as "anyone who increases by participation the concretization of the love of God in history." Koyama coins the term *neighborology* and suggests that "in order to be able to present Christ in 'neighborological' terms to our neighbor we must learn, first of all, to *see* him, whether he be Buddhist, Hindu, Moslem, animist, Communist, nationalist, revolutionary, intellectual or uneducated."[24]

Samuel Rayan of India believes that there is a latent liberation theology in all religions and for this very reason Indian christology must be open to fresh insights from Hindu, Muslim and Buddhist theologies. He adds: "We shall therefore avoid a sectarian interpretation of our history and of the gospel of Jesus, for all who work for justice are God's co-workers."[25] In his book *A Gandhian Theology of Liberation*, Ignatius Jesudasan notes how the christology of Mahatma Gandhi can be a model for Christianity's encounter with other religions. "Gandhi's Christology can be discovered in the Christian concept of service to one's fellow humans . . . for communal growth in truth, involving whole races and peoples converging in mutual recognition and love."[26] For Gandhi — as for most liberation theologians — the *descriptive* dimension of christology, enshrined in its formal dogmas, must always be of lesser import than the *prescriptive* dimension that underscores the spiritual oneness of all people.

Other Asian liberation theologians talk of the *cosmic Christ* and *the ontological universality of Christ*, and understand the importance of using symbols taken from non-Christian religions as vehicles for communication. Here once again they follow the "Christ from below" approach. This model by no means equates Christ and Buddha and Mohammed and Amos and all the other world religious figures. But this model, as C. S. Song suggests, "should not blind Christians to God's continuing presence and work outside Christianity. In fact, it should open our eyes to perceive a redemptive quality in moments and events in other cultures and histories that have to be considered substantively related to the work of Jesus Christ."[27] The work of Christ as the liberator of the human condition should provide a bridge and not a barrier to other religions.

JUSTICE AND SPIRITUALITY

This final theme may be the most important one of all, for it is the least understood. Liberation theologians speak loudly and clearly with one voice when they insist that justice and spirituality must *never* be separated. They are the convex and concave sides of the liberation lens. They constitute what is called *integral liberation*. Critics more often than not fault liberation theology for its exclusive concern for justice issues and their neglect of the spiritual or interior life. *Nothing could be further from the truth*. For liberation theologians, the two dimensions are absolutely essential ingredients in the total life of the Christian.

Gustavo Gutiérrez has been accused of politicizing the Christian faith, of reducing faith to the political arena. To be sure, Gutiérrez believes that faith cannot be divorced from the political life. But to deny faith's spiritual dimension is to misunderstand the whole point of Gutiérrez's theology of liberation. To counteract this false impression, he wrote his book, *We Drink from Our Own Wells: The Spiritual Journey of a People.* Here his goal is to show how Christian spirituality undergirds his theology of liberation. He writes: "Since the very first days of the theology of liberation, the question of spirituality (specifically: the following of Jesus) has been of deep concern. Moreover, this kind of reflection that the theology of liberation represents is conscious of the fact that it was, and continues to be, preceded by the spiritual experience of Christians who are committed to the process of liberation."[28] For Gutiérrez liberation is an all-embracing process. The mystical or contemplative life is as important as the active. One is impoverished without the other.

Segundo Galilea echoes this same conviction: "Authentic Christian contemplation, which crosses through the desert, transforms contemplatives into prophets and heroes of commitment. Christianity brings about the synthesis of the militant and the mystic, of the political and the contemplative, overcoming the false contradiction between the 'contemplative-religious' and the 'committed-militant.' "[29]

African liberation theology has underscored the importance of spirituality. As noted earlier, the independent African Christian churches have recognized the pervading spirituality of native African religion and have seen spirituality as an important implication of the presence of the Holy Spirit. Likewise, throughout Asia, spirituality is central to the indigenous religions. C. S. Song speaks of "doing theology with a third eye," a phrase he borrows from the Japanese Zen master Daisetz Suzuki. Song quotes Suzuki: "Zen wants us to open a 'third eye,' as Buddhists call it, to the hitherto unheard-of region shut away from us through our own ignorance. When the cloud of ignorance disappears, the infinity of heaven is manifested where we see for the first time into the nature of our own being."[30]

This spiritual dimension pervading all of reality can be an important meeting ground between Christian liberation theology and Eastern religions. These religions believe that the dimension of the *holy* or *sacred* permeates the human, bringing together the transcendent and the immanent in a spiritual oneness and showing the interconnectedness of all reality. Here Western classical Christianity, with its overemphasis on the rational or conceptual dimension, faces a major challenge in opening itself to the mystical dimension. Liberation theology can provide that link. Aloysius Pieris believes, for example, that the time is ripe for what he calls a "core-to-core dialogue" between Christianity and Buddhism in bringing together the dimensions of *gnosis* and *agape.* He uses the phrase "theology of double baptism," by which he means baptism both "in the Jordan of Asian religiosity and baptism in the Calvary of Asian poverty."[31] For C. S. Song, the symbol of the Buddha or Bodhisattva sitting cross-legged on the lotus is as important to a proper appreciation of Asian spirituality as the cross is to a Christian.

The point crucial to liberation theologians is that spirituality and justice must intersect. Any religion that concerns itself solely with the interior or the exterior is impoverished. There is, as Gutiérrez puts it, a "spirituality of the life of the poor," a spiritual justice which is at the heart of liberation theology. Justice based on spirituality, Gutiérrez affirms, becomes a community enterprise. "It is the passage of a people through the solitude and dangers of the desert, as it carves out its own way in the following of Jesus Christ. This spiritual exercise is the well from which we must drink."[32]

In conclusion, liberation theology issues a call not only to Christianity, but to the other religions of the world as well. Are these religions willing to show "a preferential option for the poor"? Can the communities of the poor which are irrupting throughout the Third World be the basis for a new "people's theology" which seeks to liberate humanity from all forms of oppression: poverty, servitude, racism, sexism, and the like? Can justice and spirituality become partners in a world embracing enterprise? Can the struggle for justice and belief in God come to mean one and the same thing? Herein lies the stirring challenge of third-world Christian liberation theology.

NOTES

1. *Hope and Suffering* (Grand Rapids, Michigan: William B. Eerdmans, 1984), p. 155.

2. *On Earth As It Is In Heaven: Jews, Christians and Liberation Theology* (Maryknoll, N.Y.: Orbis Books, 1987), p. 51.

3. "Profiles: Parish Priest," *The New Yorker*, 13 June, 1988, pp. 55–56.

4. *Basic Ecclesial Communities: The Evangelization of the Poor* (Maryknoll, N.Y.: Orbis Books, 1982), p. 37.

5. Ibid., p. 3.

6. "A Theology of Liberation in Asian Churches," *East Asian Pastoral Review* 23, no. 2 (1986): p. 117.

7. *Waterbuffalo Theology* (Maryknoll, N.Y.: Orbis Books, 1974), p. 84.

8. Ibid., p. vii.

9. Ibid., p. viii.

10. *The Origins and Development of African Theology* (Maryknoll, N.Y.: Orbis Books, 1985), p. 45.

11. *Polygamy Reconsidered: African Plural Marriages and the Christian Churches* (Maryknoll, N.Y.: Orbis Books, 1975), p. 206.

12. Koyama, *Waterbuffalo Theology*, p. 83.

13. Juan Luis Segundo, *The Liberation of Theology* (Maryknoll, N.Y.: Orbis Books, 1976), p. 9.

14. Gustavo Gutiérrez, *A Theology of Liberation* (Maryknoll, N.Y.: Orbis Books, 1973), pp. 26–27, p. 138.

15. Pablo Richard, ed., *The Idols of Death and the God of Life* (Maryknoll, N.Y.: Orbis Books, 1983), p. 1.

16. Ibid., p. 144.

17. Ibid., p. 202.

18. *The Compassionate God* (Maryknoll, N.Y.: Orbis Books, 1982), pp. 167–68, 160.

19. *Planetary Theology* (Maryknoll, N.Y.: Orbis Books, 1984), p. 95.

20. Song, *The Compassionate God*, p. 260.

21. *Church: Charism and Power: Liberation Theology and the Institutional Church* (New York: Crossroad, 1985), p. 23.

22. *Jesus Christ Liberator* (Maryknoll, N.Y.: Orbis Books, 1978), p. 219.

23. "Christianity and Buddhism in Core-to-Core Dialogue," *Cross Currents* 37, no. 1: pp. 74–75.

24. Koyama, *Waterbuffalo Theology*, pp. 93–94, 220.

25. "Theological Priorities in India Today," in *Irruption of the Third World*, ed. Virginia Fabella and Sergio Torres (Maryknoll, N.Y.: Orbis Books, 1983), p. 31.

26. *A Gandhian Theology of Liberation* (Maryknoll, N.Y.: Orbis Books, 1984), p. 107.

27. *Third-Eye Theology* (Maryknoll, N.Y.: Orbis Books, 1979), p. 115.

28. *We Drink from Our Own Wells* (Maryknoll, N.Y.: Orbis Books, 1984), p. 1.

29. *Following Jesus* (Maryknoll, N.Y.: Orbis Books, 1981), p. 63.

30. Song, *Third-Eye Theology*, p. 11.

31. *A Theology of Liberation in Asian Churches*, p. 45.

32. *We Drink from Our Own Wells*, p. 137.

2

Judaism and Liberation Theology

DAN COHN-SHERBOK

In the Jewish community, little notice has been taken of the emergence of liberation theology despite the fact that it is possibly the major Christian theological achievement of the twentieth century. Although Jewish-Christian dialogue has recently been undertaken worldwide, those engaged in such encounters have largely ignored this crucially significant Christian development.[1] This is regrettable since third-world theologians in Latin America, Asia, and Africa have gone back to their Jewish roots in the Hebrew Scriptures. Suddenly, Jewish and Christian writers find themselves using the same vocabulary and motifs, and this bond paves the way for a mutual examination of commonly shared religious ideals.

THE JEWISH REJECTION OF JESUS

In his overview of liberation theology Deane Ferm illustrates that this new movement offers a fresh perspective on the theological enterprise. Inspired by faith, Christian liberation theologians encourage an alternative way of thinking about God's activity in the world. As Leonardo Boff and Clodovis Boff point out, its theologians are not armchair intellectuals, but rather "organic intellectuals" (in organic communion with people) and "militant theologians," working with the poor and engaging in their pastoral responsibilities.[2] Yet, despite their radical innovations, third-world liberation theologians accept the traditional religious tenets of the Christian faith. For these writers, Jesus is the Messiah who has come to redeem the world. As God incarnate and part of the Trinity, he offers all human beings the promise of entry into the Kingdom.

For this reason, the New Testament is of fundamental significance in formulating a programme of Christian social action. In the gospels, Christ's message and ministry is proclaimed. In the words of Gustavo Gutiérrez,

"Christians are witnesses of the risen Christ. It is this testimony that calls us together in a permanent way as the church and at the same time is the very heart of the church's mission. The realization that life and not death has the final say about history is the source of the joy of believers who experience, thereby, God's unmerited love for them. To evangelize is to communicate this joy; it is to transmit, individually and as a community, the good news of God's love that has transformed our lives."[3] Such a religious commitment—which underlies the diverse strands of liberation theology emanating from South America, Asia, and Africa—obviously separates Christian liberationists from religiously devout Jews. Through the ages, Jews have attacked Christianity for its doctrine of the Incarnation. According to rabbinic sources, the belief that God was in Christ is heretical—the contention that God is both Father and Son is viewed as dualistic theology. Similarly, the doctrine of the Trinity has been bitterly denounced. Through the ages, Jewish thinkers rejected trinitarianism as incompatible with monotheism. In the Middle Ages, Jewish martyrs gave their lives rather than accept such a belief, and modern Jewish theology is equally critical of any attempt to harmonize the belief in God's unity with the doctrine of a triune God. Contemporary Jewish theologians of all degrees of observance thus affirm that Judaism is fundamentally incompatible with what they perceive as the polytheistic character of Christian belief.

Connected with the Jewish rejection of the doctrines of the Incarnation and the Trinity, Jews have consistently denied the Christian claim that Jesus is the Messiah for several important reasons. First, according to Judaism it is obvious that Jesus did not fulfill the messianic expectations. Jesus did not restore the kingdom of David to its former glory; nor did he gather the dispersed ones of Israel and restore all the laws of the Torah that were in abeyance, such as the sacrificial cult. He did not compel all Israel to walk in the way of the Torah, nor did he rebuild the Temple and usher in a new order in the world and nature.

In other words, Jesus did not inaugurate a cataclysmic change in history. Universal peace, in which there is neither war nor competition, did not come about on earth. Thus, for Jews, Jesus did not fulfill the prophetic messianic hope in a redeemer who would bring political and spiritual redemption as well as earthly blessings and moral perfection to the human race.

A second objection to Jesus' messiahship concerns the Christian claim that he possesses a special relationship with God. This notion was repeatedly stated in the gospels. In Matthew, for example, we read, "No one knows the Son except the Father; and no one knows the Father, except the Son" (Matt. 11:27). In John's Gospel, Jesus declares, "I am the way, and the truth, and the life; no one comes to the Father but by me. If you had known me, you would have known my Father also; henceforth you have known him and have seen him" (John 14:6–7). This concept undermined the Jewish conviction that God is equally near to all.

The third objection to Jesus arises from his attitude toward sin and sinners. The traditional task of the prophets was to castigate Israel for rejecting God's law, not to forgive sin. Jesus, however, took upon himself the power to do this. Thus, he declared with regard to a paralytic, " 'For which is easier to say, "Your sins are forgiven" or to say, "Rise and walk?" But that you may know the Son of man has authority on earth to forgive sins' — he then said to the paralytic: 'Rise, take up your bed and go home' " (Matt. 9:5–6). When Jesus said to the woman of ill repute, "Your sins are forgiven," his companions were shocked. "Who is this, who even forgives sins?" they asked (Luke 7:48–49). It is not surprising that this was their reaction, since such a usurpation of God's prerogative was without precedent. A similar objection applies to the gospel record that Jesus performed miracles on his own authority without making reference to God (John 5:18-21).

A fourth objection to Jesus concerns his admonition to break all human ties: "Whoever of you does not renounce all that he has cannot be my disciple" (Luke 14:33). Or again, "Who is my mother?, and who are my brothers? Here are my mother and my brothers! For whoever does the will of my Father in heaven is my brother, and sister and mother" (Matt. 12:48–50). Similarly, he declared, "Call no man your father on earth, you have one Father who is in heaven" (Matt. 23:9). In contrast to these views, Judaism asserts that persons cannot live a full life unless they are members of a family and well integrated into the larger community. The renunciation of family bonds is regarded as a travesty of the created order.

Finally, Jesus' teaching is rejected by traditional Jews because his interpretation of Jewish law is at variance with rabbinic tradition. Though, at one point in the gospels, Jesus declared that no change should be made in the law (Matt. 5:17), he disregarded a number of important precepts. Several times on the Sabbath, for example, Jesus cured individuals who were not dangerously ill, in violation of the rabbinic precept that the Sabbath law can only be broken for the saving and preserving of life (Matt. 12:9–14; Luke 13:10–16; 14:3–6). Conversely Jesus was more strict about the law of divorce than the Pharisees. He stated, "It was also said, 'Whoever divorces his wife, let him give her a certificate of divorce.' But, I say to you, that everyone who divorces his wife, except on the ground of unchastity, makes her an adulteress; and whoever marries a divorced woman commits adultery" (Matt. 5:31f.).

In a similar vein, Jesus rejected the biblical and rabbinic teaching regarding dietary laws: "Not that which entereth into the mouth defileth the man," he stated, "but what comes out of the mouth, this defiles a man" (Matt. 15:11). Another serious divergence from traditional Jewish law was Jesus' view that the ritual washing of hands before meals was unimportant. In response to the Pharisees' criticism of his disciples for eating without first washing their hands, he rebuked the Pharisees for not keeping the ethical commandments. "These are," he stated, "what defiles a man: but to eat with unwashed hands does not defile man" (Matt. 15:20).

Jesus also violated the laws regarding fasts. The gospels record that when the Pharisees were fasting, Jesus' disciples did not fast. When questioned about this, he replied, "Can the wedding guests mourn as long as the bridegroom is with them? The days will come, when the bridegroom is taken away from them, and then they will fast" (Matt. 9:15). When the Pharisees criticized the disciples for plucking wheat on the Sabbath, Jesus proclaimed, "The Son of Man is Lord of the Sabbath" (Matt. 12:8).

These objections to the traditional Christian understanding of Jesus separate the Christian faith from the Jewish tradition. For all Christians—including third-world liberationists—Jesus is Son of God; he is the awaited Messiah. As God's anointed, he ushers in the Kingdom of God in which the old Torah is superseded. He summons all to enter into a new covenant with God based on divine love and grace. To the Jewish mind, however, God's covenant with the Jews is intact. The Messiah has not yet come. As has been the case throughout Jewish history, the Jews are still obligated to keep God's commandments. Their task for the present is to become God's copartners in maintaining and preserving righteousness, justice, and peace in an as yet unredeemed world.

A NEW UNDERSTANDING OF JEWS

Although Christian liberation theologians see Jesus as Messiah and God incarnate, they repeatedly emphasize that their concern is not to theorize abstractly about christological doctrines. Such traditional theological reflection, they believe, has been misguided, since it has tended to obscure the figure of Jesus. Frequently, Christ has been reduced to a sublime abstraction, which has led to a spiritual conception of the Son of God divorced from Jesus' concrete historicity. Such a theoretically abstract presentation of Christ has also given rise to the view that Jesus was a pacificist who loved all human beings and died on behalf of all people in order to free them from sin. According to liberation theologians, such an emphasis distorts the real nature of Jesus in that it exempts him from history and uses Christianity as support for ideologies espousing peace and order.[4] Further, liberation theologians point out that if Christ is seen in absolute terms, the tendency exists to neglect earthly matters; in particular, the emphasis on the absoluteness of Christ can bring about an unquestioning acceptance of the social and political status quo.[5]

In the light of these objections to traditional Christian speculation, liberation theologians have insisted that the historical Jesus should be the starting point for christological reflection. In this endeavor, biblical hermeneutics cannot be taken to mean simply the art of understanding ancient texts; rather, it also involves an identification with Jesus' life and message. This is so, liberationists maintain, since the tradition of the primitive church preserved of Jesus only that which functioned in the life of the faith of the community. Thus, understanding of Jesus cannot be reduced to scientific investigation; instead, as Leonardo Boff explains, "to really comprehend who Jesus is, one must approach him as one touched by and attached to him. Defining Jesus we are defining ourselves. The more we know ourselves, the more we know Jesus."[6]

Following this impetus, liberation theologians see a structural similarity between the situation in Jesus' time and in the modern world. Oppression and persecution in contemporary society as in first-century Palestine, they believe, are contrary to the divine plan for humanity. In the gospels, Jesus initiated a programme of liberation; yet his struggle against the Jewish authorities illustrated the conflict that any project of liberation will provoke. The historical Jesus thus clarifies the chief elements of christological faith: by following his life and cause in one's own life, the truth of Jesus emerges. As Leonardo Boff explains, "Jesus did not present himself as the explanation of reality; he presented himself as an urgent demand for the transformation of that reality."[7] By offering a critique of humanity and society, Jesus points the way to the fulfillment of the Kingdom of God.[8]

For Jews, liberation theology thus offers a new orientation to Jesus. Previously, Jews and Christians have been unable to find common theological ground—instead of attempting to forge a bridge between the two faiths, Jews have repudiated Christian claims about Jesus' divinity while Christians have denounced Jews for their unwillingness to accept Christ as their Savior. The doctrines of the Trinity, the Incarnation and the understanding of Jesus as the Messiah have separated the two traditions and have served as stumbling blocks to fruitful interfaith encounter. Today, however, liberation theology offers a profoundly different direction to Christian thought. Unlike theologians of the past, these writers are not concerned with analyzing Jesus' dual nature as God and man; abstract speculation about the central issue of traditional christology (divine personhood and hypostatic union) has been set aside. Instead, liberation theology focuses on the historical Jesus and the starting point for Christian reflection. As Jon Sobrino writes, "Our Christology will avoid abstractionism and the attendant danger of manipulating the Christ event. The history of the church shows, from its very beginning that any focusing on the Christ of faith will jeopardize the very essence of the Christian faith if it neglects the historical Jesus."[9]

What is of crucial significance for Jewish-Christian dialogue is that the primary emphasis here on understanding Jesus himself provides the basis for the formulation of Christian theology. The historical context of the gospels is in this way reclaimed for Christians, and Jesus' teaching in the New Testament is related directly to God's design as recorded in the Old Testament. In particular, Jesus is viewed as following in the footsteps of the great prophets of ancient Israel. As Ignacio Ellacuría insists, prophecy in the Old Testament and Jesus' mission in the New Testament must be related. "The prophecy of the Old Testament," he writes, "takes on its full ascendent import only in terms of what Jesus himself represents. By the same token the meaning of Jesus himself would escape us if we disregarded the history of prophecy."[10]

From an historical standpoint, then, the picture of Jesus that emerges from the gospel narratives is inextricably connected to this Jewish background. The consequence of this for Jews is profound, for it opens the way to a fresh vision of Jesus' mission. His criticism of the religious establishment, like that of the pre-exilic prophets, should be understood not as a rejection of Judaism itself, but as a call to the nation to return to the God of their fathers. Seen in this manner, Jesus' teaching stands in the tradition of the ethical prophets of ancient Israel, and it is to the prophetic books of the Bible that we must turn to find the crucial links that relate Jesus to his Jewish past. In this context, the Jew can recognize Jesus as following the prophetic tradition, even though he cannot say with the Christian liberation theologian that Jesus is "God of God, light of light, very God of very God, begotten not made, being of one substance with the Father."

THE KINGDOM OF GOD

Liberation theologians insist that the Kingdom of God as understood by Jesus is not the denial of history, but the elimination of its corruptibility. In the words of José Míguez Bonino, "God builds His Kingdom from and within human history and its entirety; his action is a constant call and challenge to men. Man's response is realized in the concrete area of history with its economic, political and ideological options."[11] The growth and ultimate fulfillment of the Kingdom rests on a struggle against exploitation, alienation, oppression, and persecution; it embraces all: the world, society, and the individual. It is this totality which is to be transformed through the activity that God has initiated but not yet fully completed.

Within this unfolding of God's eschatological scheme, liberation theologians maintain that Christians have a crucial role. It is the responsibility of each person to engage in the quest for the liberation of the oppressed — this is a task which obliges all Christians to offer assistance not only in the religious and spiritual domain, but in the sphere of politics, economics, and culture. According to Pierre Bigo, "It is not enough to say that doing so is a condition for salvation; it is the very coming of the Kingdom in its temporal form."[12] The way of the Kingdom implies the building of a just society. As Gutiérrez notes, a situation of injustice is incompatible with the Kingdom: "the building of a just society has worth in terms of the Kingdom, or in more current phraseology, to participate in the process of liberation is already in a certain sense, a salvific work."[13] Entrance into the Kingdom is open only to those who practice justice and distribute to the poor whatever they have over and above their real needs.

The heart of the gospel message is subversive; it embodies the Israelite hope in the end of the domination of human beings over one another. The struggle for the establishment of God's Kingdom involves the overthrow of established powers—political involvement is imperative. To know God is to be concerned for the creation of a new order regulated by the principle of love. In the words of M. Echegoyen:

> Our hope may refer to the Kingdom, to the second coming of Christ but it begins here and now, in this society in which I happen to live and for whose transformation—humanization—I am inescapably responsible. Loving one's neighbor, which is the first commandment by definition, today means working to change the structures that can destroy my neighbor, the people, the poor.[14]

For liberation theologians, such change involves the eradication of poverty which is incompatible with a Kingdom of love and justice. Some theologians even go so far as to advocate the necessity of violent revolution as a means of altering the economic structures of society.[15]

In the writings of these theologians, then, there is a common conviction that the rights of the poor must be upheld in a quest for the liberation of the oppressed. Peace, justice, love, and freedom are dominating motifs in their understanding of the coming of God's Kingdom. Breaking with traditional Christian theology, liberation theologians emphasize that these are not internal attitudes—they are social realities that need to be implemented in human history. Gutiérrez eloquently formulates this shift away from the values of the past: "A poorly understood spiritualization," he writes, "has often made us forget the human consequences of the eschatological promises and the power to transform unjust social structures which they imply. The elimination of misery and exploitation is a sign of the coming of the Kingdom."[16] Thus, the Kingdom of God, contrary to what many Christians believe, does not signify something that is outside this world. It involves the effort of each individual to bring about a new order, a mission based on Jesus' actions and teachings as recorded in the gospels.

What is of central importance for Christian-Jewish encounter is the liberationist's insistence that the coming of the Kingdom involves individual participation in the creation of a new world. Though Judaism rejects the Christian claim that Jesus has ushered in the period of messianic redemption, Jews have steadfastly adhered to the belief that God is a supreme ruler who calls all people to join him in bringing about the Kingdom of God on earth. This understanding is an essential element of Psalmist theology, and it is a central theological motif of the old Testament. In later rabbinic literature, this vision of the human role in bringing about God's Kingdom is elaborated further.

According to the rabbis, the Kingdom of God takes place in this world; it is established by humanity's obedience to the divine will. The Kingdom of God consists in a complete moral order on earth—the reign of trust, righteousness, and holiness among all people and nations. The fulfillment of this conception ultimately rests with the coming of the Messiah; nevertheless, it is one's duty to participate in the creation of a better world in anticipation of the messianic redemption. In the words of the rabbis, "Man is a co-worker with God in the work of creation."[17]

According to rabbinic theology, human beings are the center of creation, for it is only they among all created beings who can, through righteousness, make the Kingdom glorious.[18] In rabbinic midrash, the view is expressed that God's Kingship did not come into operation until humans were created: "When the Holy One, blessed be He, consulted the Torah as to the creation of the world, he answered, 'Master of the world, if there be no host, over whom will the King reign, and if there be no peoples praising him, where is the glory of the King?' "[19] It is only human beings who can act as his copartners in perfecting the world. What God requires is obedience to his ways of righteousness and justice: "You are my lovers and friends." "You walk in my ways," God declares to Israel. "As the Omnipotent is merciful and gracious, long-suffering and abundant in goodness so should you be feeding the hungry, giving drink to the thirsty, clothing the naked, ransoming the captives, and marrying the orphans."[20] Throughout biblical and rabbinic literature, Jews were encouraged to strive for the highest conception of life in which the rule of truth, righteousness, and holiness would be established among humankind. Such a desire is the eternal hope of God's people—a longing for God's Kingdom as expressed in the daily liturgy of the synagogue. Here we can see the point of intersection between the Jewish faith and Christian liberation theology. For both Jews and liberation theologians, the coming of the Kingdom in which God's heavenly rule will be made manifest is a process in which all human beings have a role. It involves the struggle for the reign of justice and righteousness on earth. The Kingdom is not, as has been the case in traditional Christianity, an internalized, spiritualized, other-worldly conception. Rather, it involves human activity in a historical context. Drawing on the Hebrew Scriptures and the New Testament, liberation theologians have attempted to demonstrate the tasks Christians must undertake in the building of the Kingdom. Similarly, the rabbis elaborated the teaching of the Torah about men and women's partnership with God in bringing God's rule. For both faiths, the moral life is at the center of the unfolding of God's plan for humanity. Such a shared vision should serve to unite Jews and Christians in a joint undertaking to transform our imperfect world in anticipation of the divine promise of the eschatological fulfillment at the end of time.

THE EXODUS

For liberation theologians, Jesus is the liberator who paves the way for the realization of the Kingdom of God on earth. In presenting this message of hope, liberation theologians repeatedly emphasize the centrality of the exodus from Egypt. "The Exodus experience," Gutiérrez writes, "is paradigmatic. It remains vital and contemporary due to similar historical experiences which the People of God undergo. It structures our faith in the gift of the Father's love. In Christ and through the Spirit, men are becoming one in the very heart of history."[21] Thus, these Christian theologians look to the history of the Jewish people for inspiration in their struggle against exploitation and oppression in contemporary society, and this divine act of redemption of the Israelite nation provides a basis for a critique of traditional Christian thought and modern society.[22]

Liberation theologians stress that the exodus was not simply an event in the history of the Jewish people; instead, it evoked a deep response on the part of the descendants of those who had been liberated. As J. Severino Croatto writes, "The word, Exodus, was 'recharged' with fresh meanings by successive hermeneutical re-readings up to the time that it was fixed permanently as expressing a whole worldview in the Exodus account in its present form."[23] The profundity of the exodus, therefore, consists in its significance for later generations; the past holds a promise for those who understand its relevance. The exodus is fraught with meaning. For third-world theologians, it is an account of liberations of oppressed peoples, and using this framework, they believe it is possible to understand the plight of those who are presently afflicted from the perspective of the biblical exodus—the situation of peoples in economic, political, social, or cultural "bondage."[24]

In this context, liberation theologians stress the crucial role of Moses in the process of liberation. Enrique Dussel, for example, begins his study of the history and theology of liberation by focusing on Moses' call to lead his people out of captivity.[25] Moses had fled to the desert because he had killed an Egyptian. He lived comfortably as a herdsman with his wife, his father-in-law, and his flocks. But, one day he heard God speak to him out of a bush. "Moses, Moses," God cried, "I have seen the affliction of my people who are in Egypt, and have heard their cry because of their taskmasters; I know their sufferings, and I have come down to deliver them out of the hands of the Egyptians. Come, I will send you to Pharaoh that you may bring forth my people, the sons of Israel, out of Egypt" (Exod. 3:7–10). This divine encounter is represented by Dussel as follows:[26]

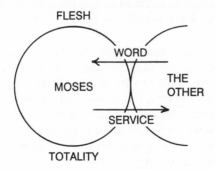

Here God, the Other, reveals himself to Moses: Moses heard God's Word, "Liberate my people out of Egypt." Established in the totality of fleshly, daily life, Moses responded by serving as the liberator of his people. We, too, are being called continually, Dussel contends, but we do not hear anything. Yet, like Moses, we must awaken ourselves to the divine command. As Dussel writes, "God keeps on revealing himself to us as the Other who summons us. He is the first Other. If I do not listen to my fellowmen in bondage, then I am not listening to God either."[27]

Liberation theologians also utilize the exodus narrative to explain that God guides the destiny of the persecuted. In the flight from Egypt, the Bible stresses that God leads the people; he did not take them out by way of the land of the Philistines, although that was near, for God said, "Let the people repent when they see war and return to Egypt. But, God led the people round by way of the wilderness towards the Red Sea" (Exod. 13:17–18). When the Egyptian army attempted to capture the Israelites, God intervened and saved them. Once Israel had crossed the Red Sea, God sustained them in their wanderings: God gave them sweet water at Marah, sent them manna and quail in the desert, gave them safe passage through the Transjordan, and delivered the Amorite kings into the hands of the Israelites. God not only delivered and protected God's people, but also led them to their own land where they were no longer oppressed. Before Moses' death, God proclaimed to Joshua, "I myself will be with you" as God was with Moses. The conquest is thus the second stage of God's deliverance, and even the prostitute of Jericho knows that God will take the side of God's people, just as in the past: "I know that the Lord has given you the land. We have heard how the Lord dried up the water of the Red Sea before you when you came out of Egypt" (Josh. 2:9–10).

Thus, it is clear that the exodus experience is typologically significant for liberation theologians; it is a paradigm of divine liberation of the oppressed and persecuted. And, just as the exodus is a key element in liberation theology, so it has been in the self-understanding of the Jewish people through the centuries. In the biblical period, details of the exodus were recorded in cultic sayings, in Wisdom literature, and by the prophets. After the exile, the exodus continued to play a dominant role in the Jewish faith. In particular, the festival of Passover was regarded as crucially important in the religious life of the people. As Louis Finkelstein remarks:

The Passover celebration commemorates an event which will probably symbolize for all time the essential meaning of freedom, namely freedom devoted to a purpose. When Israel came forth from bondage, it was not simply to enjoy liberty, but to make of liberty an instrument of service. The Israelites alone made the moment of their origin as a people one of permanent self-dedication to the principle of universal freedom as the essential prerequisite for spiritual growth. Hence, the event has meaning for all living peoples.[28]

In post-Enlightenment Judaism, modern Jewish writers have emphasized the significance of the themes of liberty, redemption, and freedom as found in the Passover festival. Franz Rosenzweig, for example, argued that there is an intrinsic connection between the Passover and the Sabbath. The Sabbath, he maintained, is a reminder of the exodus from Egypt: "The freedom of the man servant and the maid servant which it proclaims is conditioned by the deliverance of the people as a people from the servitude of Egypt. And in every command to respect the freedom of even the man servant, or even the alien among the people, the law of God renews the awareness of the connection holding between the freedom within the people, a freedom decreed by God, and the freeing of the people from Egyptian servitude, a liberation enacted by God."[29] Furthermore, the Passover meal is a symbol of Israel's vocation as a people; the deliverance of the nation affords a glimpse of its destiny. It is not only today that enemies rise up against the Jews, they have arisen in every generation, and God has always taken the side of the chosen people as long as they remained faithful to the divine covenant. All this points to the ultimate redemption, as prophesied by Isaiah, of the day when the wolf shall dwell with the lamb and the world shall be as full of the knowledge of the Lord as the sea is of water.[30]

The moral implications of the redemption from Egypt are emphasized in *The Ethics of Judaism* by Moritz Lazarus. The exodus, he writes, has a predominant place in the biblical and rabbinic cycle of religious ideas. The most exalted moral statutes in the Torah concerning the treatment of strangers are connected with the exodus, and are, from a psychological point of view, impressively inculcated by means of the injunction, "You know the heart of the stranger." The prophets and the psalmists employ this event to illustrate God's providence and grace, and the rabbis deduce from it the two fundamental aspects of Jewish ethics: the notion of liberty and the ethical task. Throughout the history of Judaism, Lazarus writes, "the notion of liberty, inner, moral, and spiritual liberty, cherished as a pure, exalted ideal, possible only under and through the Law, was associated with the memory of the redemption from Egyptian slavery, and this memory in turn was connected with symbolic practices accompanying every act, pleasure, and celebration."[31]

Kaufmann Kohler, a leading Reform theologian, saw in the Passover a symbol of thanksgiving and hope that sustained the Jewish nation in their tribulations: "The Passover festival with its 'night of divine watching' endowed the Jew ever anew with endurance during the dark night of medieval tyranny and with faith in 'the Keeper of Israel who slumbereth not nor sleepeth.' " Moreover, he believed that the feast of redemption promises a day of liberty to those who continue to struggle under oppression and exploitation: the modern Jew can see in the reawakening of his religious and social life in Western lands the token of the future liberation of all humankind. "The Passover feast," he states, "brings him the clear and hopeful message for humanity from all bondage of today and of spirit."[32]

In *Judaism as Life and Creed*, Morris Joseph focuses on the contemporary significance of Passover. It is, he believes, the greatest of all the historical festivals in that it brings the Jew into close contact with the past. No other festival, he contends, so powerfully appeals to historical sympathies. At the Passover ceremony, the Jew is at one with his redeemed ancestors, sharing with them the consciousness of their freedom, their sense of nationality that is beginning to stir in their ears. "He shares," he writes, "their glowing hopes, the sweet joy of newly discovered manhood." Through God's redemption, the Israelites were able to free themselves from despair, and they share in this deliverance. "We march forth," he states, "with them from the scenes of oppression in gladness and gratitude. The ideal of the rabbis fulfills itself. 'In every generation it is for the Jew to think that he himself went forth from Egypt' (Pesahim 10:5)."[33]

Ahad Ha-Am concentrates on Moses the liberator as an ideal type of hero. Moses, he points out, was neither a warrior nor a statesman. Instead, he was a prophet who put justice into action. Confronted by acts of iniquity, he took the side of the victim. The early events of his life in which he struggled against injustice served as a prelude to his revolt against Egyptian oppression.

> That great moment dawned in the wilderness, far from the turmoil of life. The prophet's soul is weary of the endless struggle, and longs for peace and rest. He seeks the solitude of the shepherd's life, goes into the wilderness with his sheep, and reaches Horeb, the mountain of the Lord. But even here he finds no rest. He feels in his innermost being that he has not yet fulfilled his mission. Suddenly, the prophet hears the voice of the Lord, the voice he knows so well calling to him from some forgotten corner of his innermost being: "I am the God of their fathers. I have surely seen the affliction of My people that are in Egypt. Come now, therefore, and I will send thee unto Pharaoh, that thou mayest bring forth My people the children of Israel out of Egypt."[34]

In the account of the exodus from Egypt, therefore, the faith of Israel is portrayed as a response to God's will. What is required of Israel is obedient participation in the act of emancipation. For liberation theologians, this biblical anchorage leads to a practical orientation of the faith: praxis, rather than theological reflection, is understood as the key to Christian witness. Liberation theologians stress that theology must start from actions committed to the process of liberation; theology is conceived as a critical reflection on praxis. For Jews, this emphasis on the concrete dimension of faith is vital. The Jewish hope lies in God's rule on earth. This is the goal of the history of the world in which the Jewish people have a central role. Throughout the Bible and in rabbinic literature, ethical behavior is the predominant theme. By doing God's will, the Jew can help to complete God's work of creation. As in the case of liberation theology, the Jewish religion focuses on orthopraxis rather than theological orthodoxy. Theological speculation is not seen as authoritative; instead, moral praxis is at the core of the faith. Deeds of goodness rather than dogma take precedence; in this, Jews and Christian liberation theologians are united in the quest for the total elimination of human wickedness.

AREAS OF SOCIAL CONCERN

This shared vision, then, can serve as a bridge between the two traditions. Liberation theology's return to traditional Jewish ideals should make it possible for both faiths to work together as never before in areas of social concern. In this quest, liberation theologians have paved the way for such common endeavor by explaining how ethical values rooted in the Bible can be put into practice. Liberation theologians repeatedly emphasize the importance of building a more just order. Recognizing the existence of class conflict, they advocate the abolition of its causes. In particular, they seek to restructure the socioeconomic foundations of society. What is needed, they believe, is a more egalitarian structure. According to these writers, unbridled capitalism is responsible for numerous ills that afflict society: marginal living and alienation; excessive inequality between different social classes; the continuing and increasing frustration of people's expectations; the unjust exercise of repressive power by domination and rules; tensions resulting from the dependence of countries on other centers of economic power; growing imbalance and perversion of international trade; the flight of economic and human resources; the evasion of taxes by various countries; international monopolies and the imperialism of money.

To escape from these evils, liberation theologians contend that a major transformation must take place. The Christian community must press for the adoption of socialist principles and policies. Such a programme would ideally result in a more equal distribution of goods and services. Many Jews today would welcome such reforms. No doubt they would reject both a full-fledged socialist state along Marxist-Leninist lines as well as violent revolution, but the infusion of socialist ideals into society would, for a considerable number, evoke a positive response. For these Jews, the need to provide an adequate standard of living for everyone is of central importance. There is every reason to believe that such Jews, inspired by the social message of the Bible, could join ranks with Christian liberation theologians in the quest for equality, justice, and unity. Drawing inspiration from their shared traditions, they could subscribe to the urgent needs of all humankind.

For liberation theologians, the poor are the starting point of theological reflection rather than abstract metaphysical theories; the view "from below" is essential. Liberation theology claims that it is in the situation of the poor that God is to be found; as in Scripture, God is the Savior of the enslaved.

What is required, then, is solidarity as a protest against the poverty in which they are forced to live. As Gutiérrez explains, it is a "way of identifying oneself with the interests of the oppressed classes and challenging the exploitation that victimized them."[35] Poverty is something to be fought against and destroyed; God's salvation is achieved in the process of liberation. The problems and struggles of the poor are our own. The vocation of every person is to opt for human love and compassion. As Cussianovich explains, "Solidarity with the poor implies a commitment to turn human love into a collective experience from which there is no turning back."[36]

As God's suffering servant through the ages, the Jewish people should find this message of solidarity with the poor of paramount significance. In the Bible, the prophets condemned every kind of abuse. Scripture speaks of positive action to prevent poverty from becoming widespread. In Leviticus and Deuteronomy, there is detailed legislation designed to prevent the accumulation of wealth and the consequent exploitation of the unfortunate. Jews should thus feel an obligation to take steps to eradicate poverty and suffering from the modern world. In particular, they should address themselves to the economic deprivation that affects various groups: the young who are frustrated by the lack of opportunity to obtain training and work; laborers who are frequently ill paid and find difficulty in defending their rights; the unemployed who are discarded because of the harsh exigencies of economic life; and the old who are often marginalized and disregarded. In all such cases, the Jewish people who have consistently endured hardship should feel drawn to the downtrodden of modern society, sharing in their distress.

In pleading the case of the poor, liberation theologians have focused on the plight of the oppressed in the Third World. The underdevelopment of the poor countries, they point out, is the consequence of the development of other countries. In the words of Gutiérrez, "The dynamics of the capitalist economy lead to the establishment of a center and a periphery, simultaneously generating progress and growing wealth for the few and social imbalances, political tensions, and poverty for the many."[37] Such countries as those in Latin America were born in this context; they emerged as dependent societies in consequence of economic exploitation. Such unequal structures dominate and determine the character of the particular cultures of these countries, and they necessitate a defence of the status quo. Even modernization and the introduction of a greater rationality into the economies of these societies is required by the vested interests of the dominant groups. Imperialism and decolonization are the hallmarks of the past and present economic climate. From a cultural point of view as well, such imbalance between "developed" and "underdeveloped" countries is acute. The "underdeveloped" areas are always far away from the cultural level of the industrialized centers.

The perception of the fact of this dependence and its consequences has made it possible to formulate a policy of reform. According to liberation theology, human freedom cannot be brought about by a developmentalist approach that maintains elitism. Instead, liberationists grapple with the existing relationships based on injustice in a global frame. By analyzing the mechanisms that are being used to keep the poor of the world under domination, liberation theologians assert that authentic development can only take place if the domination of the great capitalistic countries is eliminated. What is required is a transformation that will radically change the conditions in which the poor live. In this process, human beings are seen as assuming conscious responsibility for their own destiny. As Gutiérrez explains, "This understanding provides a dynamic context and broadens the horizons of the desired social changes. In this perspective the unfolding of all of man's dimensions is demanded, a man who makes himself throughout his life and throughout history. The gradual conquest of true freedom leads to the creation of a new man and a qualitatively different society."[38]

These themes of liberation and emancipation should have important resonances for the Jewish community. As we have seen, the biblical narrative portrays the ancient Israelites as an oppressed nation redeemed by God. Throughout history, the Jewish people have been God's suffering servant, despised and rejected of men, smitten and afflicted. Through such suffering, Jews are able to gain a sympathetic awareness of the situation of others. The lesson of the Passover is at the heart of Jewish aspirations for all people, as we read in the Passover liturgy: "May He who broke Pharaoh's yoke forever shatter all fetters of oppression and hasten the day when swords shall, at last, be broken and wars ended. Soon may He call the glad tidings of redemption to be heard in all lands, so that mankind, freed from violence and from wrong, and united in an eternal covenant of brotherhood, may celebrate the universal Passover in the name of our God of freedom."[39] In this spirit, it is possible for Jews to heed the plea of the downtrodden in the Third World as well as the cry of the Palestinian people; linked with liberationists, they can press for a restructuring of the socioeconomic sphere. By combatting the worst elements of capitalism, it is possible for both Jews and Christians to participate in the struggle to bring about a better way of life.

This preoccupation with the Third World does not preclude concern for the oppressed in the first-world countries. Liberation theologians stress that in the First World there are also grave inequalities between the rich and the poor. Despite the higher general standard of living in these countries, many individuals neverthelesss suffer from substandard living conditions, poor health, concern about jobs, and constant worry about money. Further, as Lee Cormie points out, "the epidemic rate of alcoholism and other forms of drug abuse, or rape, wife beating, child abuse, and other forms of violence, of psychosomatic diseases like certain kinds of ulcers and heart disease, suggest the depths of anguish and alienation which many experience in our society."[40] According to liberation theology, there are essentially two different segments in the labor market: primary sector jobs involving high wages, good working conditions, employment stability, and job security; and secondary sector jobs involving low wages, poor working conditions, harsh and arbitrary discipline, and little opportunity for advancement.[41]

Consumerism is a dominant ideology that contributes to such inequality. The most important questions are frequently concerned with how to save on taxes and where to get the best price for goods. As Dorothee Sölle explains:

> This attempt to focus our interest and life priorities on hair spray, cat food and travelling to the Virgin Islands represents an assault on the One in whose image I am created. It is an assault on human dignity. Consumerism means that my eyes are offended, my ears are obstructed, and my hands are robbed of their creativity.[42]

Exploitation in the First World is thus different from what is found in third-world countries. Inhabitants of the first-world nations have become

> enmeshed in a cultural system that frequently perceives value in quantitative economic terms with an emphasis on having rather than being. Such hedonistic tendencies, generated by fiercely competitive economic interest, tends to divide the affluent from the poor. And nowhere is this more apparent than in the situation of the black community. In the United States, for example, as Cormie explains, slavery did not disappear with the disintegration of the plantation economy; in the period after the Civil War most blacks were relegated to work as sharecroppers. And even after the expansion of Northern industries, most blacks were channelled into the least desirable jobs and forced to live in dilapidated city areas. Only a minority of blacks have been able to gain access to the privileges and status promised by the American dream.[43]

Having once labored under the Egyptian yoke as slaves of Pharaoh, Jews today should be able to sympathize with the plight of such underprivileged sectors in the First World. In these countries, as in the Third World, the gap between the rich and the poor needs to be bridged, and facing such a challenge, Jews should be able to unite with liberationists. The attempt to build a more just society should propel Jews into the vanguard of those who attempt to restructure institutions along more egalitarian lines. By putting themselves in the shoes of the disadvantaged, Jews can envisage what life must be for the underprivileged. In this way Jews can bring to the community policies of caring and sharing; this is theology "from below," from the standpoint of those who are neglected and marginalized. By bringing their suffering to bear on these problems, the Jewish community can make a major contribution to the redemption of the poor.

In connection with this discussion of first-world poverty, liberation the-

ology has focused on life in the inner city. Here the distinction between
the powerful and the powerless is most clearly evident; in the cities, as
opposed to the suburbs, are to be found the unemployed, families unable
to cope, single-parent families, people on part-time jobs, individuals on
welfare, dropouts, and recent immigrants. In the words of John Vincent,
"These are the people in the area of your town you don't go to, the place
you pass through to get to city or suburb, the place you keep your children
away from, the place you pray for, thanking God you do not belong there."[44]
In such sections, inhabitants are divorced from the powerful forces that
shape their lives: the inner city is the place of failure and hopelessness.
The graphic social divide between the rich and the poor is an everyday
reality for those who live in large metropolitan centers. All too often, the
poverty of the inner city is the converse side of middle-class suburban life.
In the elaborate hierarchy of wealth and esteem, the situation of the poor
is an integral part. The existence of rich suburbs is linked to the presence
of ghettos and marginal sectors.

What is needed to remedy this situation is a new consciousness, an
awareness of the calamities of inner-city deprivation. First-world theologians influenced by liberation theology contend that the proper Christian
response is to engage in urban mission. By ministering to those at the
bottom of society, Christians can affirm that God is concerned with the
plight of those facing adversity. Such activity constitutes an acted parable
of the Kingdom, bringing into focus the meaning of the gospel. Such a
parable declares that the Christian cause is served best, not by places of
power and influence, but by situations of vulnerability and powerlessness.
According to liberationists, Christ is incarnate to the inner city. In his own
time, he belonged to the lower end of society; in today's world, he is to be
found also among the lowly. Urban mission thus aims to discover Jesus'
message in the economic and cultural impoverishment of the city life; from
his vantage point, the Christian can strive to ameliorate the conditions of
the downtrodden.

In pursuit of this goal, Jews, too, can enter into the life of the inner city.
Here they can embark on a task of reconstruction and restoration. Remem-
bering their sojourn in the land of Egypt, they can identify with the impoverished; by going into the city, Jews can work alongside and for the
betterment of the poor. The facts of the inner city demand such commitment to change, and in this vocation liberationists can stand shoulder to
shoulder with their Jewish brothers and sisters. Through urban mission,
Jews and Christians can affirm that hope for the modern world lies in a
sympathetic response and dedication to the weak. Beginning at the bottom,
it is possible to work for the creation of a community in which all people
are able to regain their sense of pride and self-fulfillment. By laboring
together in the neediest areas, the two faiths can join forces to bring about
God's Kingdom on earth.

As liberation theologians have noted, the unemployed are generally found in the destitute parts of the inner city. Unemployment continues to be a growing problem, and it is to this deprived group as well that liberationists have directed attention. Gutiérrez, for example, stresses that the church has an obligation to those who are without work. They constitute a pastoral and theological focus. Christians must labor on behalf of the "underemployed and unemployed, who are dismissed because of the harsh exigencies of economic crises, and often because of development models that subject workers and their families to cold economic calculations."[45] Such individuals face particular difficulties in coping with their misfortunes. With no jobs, the unemployed do not know what to do with their time, and as a consequence, they are left unfulfilled in the essential areas of basic human needs, for human relationship, for financial income, for social status and identity, and for satisfaction and fulfillment.

Helping those faced with such difficulties should be a high priority. In this, the Jewish community together with concerned Christians can take a lead in attempting to assist those out of work. Recently, Christian writers have made a number of important suggestions about the kinds of activity that could be undertaken: ways must be sought for creating new work opportunities; labor not traditionally regarded as paid work, such as housework, must be accepted as valid and necessary; new manufacturing enterprises which stimulate the job market should be encouraged; apprenticeship for the young needs to be introduced; jobs need to be spread more through job sharing and part-time work; education must be seen as a legitimate means of helping those in need.[46] In the quest to alleviate distress and disillusionment, Jews and Christians can make substantial contributions to those on the bottom of the social scale. Such a liberation from frustration and disappointment involves a reappraisal of life and labor: it is a task which can bind together both faiths in the quest for a meaningful life for all.

Liberation theology has also been concerned about the plight of women. Feminist theologians, in particular, have attempted to delineate the biblical traditions encapsulating the liberating experiences and visions of the people of Israel so as to free women from oppressive sexist structures, institutions, and internalized values. In the view of these writers, women have been and continue to be socialized into subservient roles. Either they are forced into domestic labor, or they hold badly paid jobs. Only seldom do a few women manage to occupy jobs in male professions. According to Rosemary Radford Ruether, "Work segregation is still the fundamental pattern of society. Women's work universally is regarded as of low status and prestige, poorly paid, with little security, generally of a rote and menial character. The sexist structuring of society means the elimination of women from those activities that allow for and express enhancement and development of the self, its artistic, intellectual and leadership capacities."[47] Throughout society, these theologians maintain, the full humanity of women is distorted, diminished and denied.

To restore women's self-respect, liberationists focus on God's defense and vindication of a new age in which iniquity will be overcome. Feminist theology applies the message of the prophets to the situation of women; the critique of hierarchy thus becomes a critique of patriarchy. For these writers, images of God must include feminine roles and experiences, and language about God must be transformed. For Christians, they believe it is necessary to move beyond the typology of Christ and the church as representing the dominant male and submissive female roles. Within church structures, women must be given full opportunities to participate at every level, including the ministry. In the civil sphere, too, women must be granted full equality before the law, a stance which calls for the repeal of all discriminatory legislation. There must be equal pay for equal work and full access to the professions. Many liberationists also insist on women's right to reproduction, self-defense, sex education, birth control, and abortion, as well as protection against sexual harassment, wife-beating, rape, and pornography.

In the Jewish community, there has similarly been a growing awareness of discrimination against women. Over the last two decades, a significant number of Jewish feminists have attempted to restructure the position given to women in traditional Judaism. In the past, Jewish women were not directly involved with most Jewish religious activity. Today, however, Jewish women are trying to find ways to live as full Jews. In their attempt to reconcile Judaism and feminism, these women are rediscovering various aspects of Jewish life: some study the place of women in Jewish history; others examine religious texts for clues to women's influence on Jewish life; while others redefine and feminize certain features of the Jewish tradition. In seeking equal access with men, these feminists stress that women should be allowed to participate in the areas from which they have previously been excluded: for example, serving as witnesses in a religious court, initiating divorce proceedings, acting as part of a quorum for prayer, receiving rabbinic training and ordination, as well as qualifying as cantors. For these Jewish feminists, all formal distinction between men and women in the religious as well as the secular sphere should be abolished. As S. Schneider explains, "We have been trying to take charge of events in our own lives and in every area of what we call Jewish life: religion, the community, the family, and all our interpersonal relations."[48] Given this impetus to liberate women from the restrictions of patriarchal structures, there is every reason for Jewish and Christian feminists to share their common concerns.

Not only do liberation theologians advocate a programme of liberation for all humankind, they also draw attention to human responsibility for the environment: ecological liberation is an important element in their policy of emancipation. Ever since the scientific revolution, nature has been secularized; no corner of the natural world has been immune from human control. Yet, in this expansion of material productivity, the earth has been exploited to such a degree that pollution, famine, and poverty threaten the very existence of the human race. In this light, liberationists assert that human beings must accept responsibility for the environment. In the words of Ruether, "The privilege of intelligence is not a privilege to alienate and dominate the world without concern for the welfare of all other forms of life. On the contrary, it is the responsibility to become the caretaker and cultivator of the whole ecological community upon which our existence depends. We need to remake the earth in a way that converts our minds to nature's logic of ecological harmony. This will necessarily be a new synthesis, a new creation in which human nature and nonhuman nature become friends in the creating of a livable and sustainable cosmos."[49]

Such reform calls for changed attitudes to the natural world; liberationists argue that human beings must accept that balance in nature is an essential characteristic of the earth's ecosystem. Human intervention inevitably upsets such a natural balance; thus, steps must continually be taken to restore equilibrium to the earth. In particular, environmentalists point out that care must be taken about the use of pesticides. Habitations previously available to many living creatures have been destroyed; for agricultural purposes, diversity within nature should be maintained and this requires a careful monitoring of the use of chemical substances. Pollution, too, has been regarded as a major problem in the modern world; industry, urban waste, and motor transport have all adversely affected the environment, and conservationists maintain that adequate control must be exercised over the use of pollutants that infect air and water resources. Furthermore, environmentalists contend that human beings must take steps to preserve endangered species and avoid inflicting cruelty on wild and domestic animals. In all these endeavors, there is a role for the Jewish community; the recognition that humanity is part of the ecological whole is fundamental to Jewish thought. According to the Jewish faith, humanity has been given authority over nature, and such responsibility should curb the crude exploitation of the earth for commercial purposes. Such a divine fiat should foster a sympathetic understanding of the whole ecological situation, engendering for Jews as for Christians an attitude of caring concern for all of God's creation.

These, then, are some of the areas in which Jews can unite with Christian liberation theologians to bring about God's Kingdom. In pursuit of a common goal of freedom from oppression, committed Jews and Christians can become a saving remnant in the modern world, embodying the liberation message of Scripture. Like Abraham, they can hope against hope in laboring to build a more just and human world. In the words of Helder Camara, they can become an Abrahamic minority, attentive to the cry of oppression:

> We are told that Abraham and other patriarchs heard the voice of God. Can we also hear the Lord's call? We live in a world where millions of our fellow men live under inhuman conditions, practically in slavery. If we are not deaf we hear the cries of the oppressed. Their

cries are the voice of God. We, who live in rich countries where there are always pockets of underdevelopment and wretchedness, hear if we want to hear, the unvoiced demands of those who have no voice and no hope. The pleas of those who have no voice and hope are the voice of God.[50]

CONCLUSION

Throughout history, the Jewish people have been God's suffering servant. Learning from this experience and inspired by a vision of God's reign on earth, they have an obligation to transcend their own misfortunes in attempting to ameliorate the lot of others. In the contemporary world, where Jews are often comfortable and affluent, this prophetic message of liberation can too easily be forgotten. Christian third-world liberation theology, however, with its focus on the desperate situation of those at the bottom of society, can act as a clarion to the Jewish community, awakening the people of Israel to their divinely appointed task. The Jewish tradition points to God's Kingdom as the goal and hope of humankind, a world in which all people and nations shall turn away from iniquity and injustice. This is not the hope of bliss in a future life, but the building up of the divine Kingdom of truth and peace among all peoples. As Isaiah declared, "I will also give thee for a light to the nations, that my salvation may be unto the end of the earth" (Isa. 49:6). In this mission, the people of Israel and Christian liberationists can join ranks: championing the cause of the oppressed, afflicted, and persecuted, both faiths can unite in common cause and fellowship, proclaiming together the ancient message of the Jewish liturgy in their struggle to create a better world:

O Lord our God, impose Thine awe upon all Thy works, and let Thy dread be upon all Thou hast created, that they may all form one single band to do Thy will with a perfect ear. Our God and God of our fathers, reveal Thyself in Thy splendor as King over all the inhabitants of the world, that every handiwork of Thine may know that Thou hast made it, and every creature may acknowledge that Thou hast created it, and whatsoever hath breath in its nostrils may say: the Lord God of Israel is King, and His dominion ruleth over all.[51]

NOTES

1. Marc Ellis, *Toward a Theology of Jewish Liberation* (Maryknoll, N.Y.: Orbis Books, 1987) is an exception.

2. Leonardo and Clodovis Boff, *Introducing Liberation Theology* (Maryknoll, N.Y.: Orbis Books, 1988), pp. 19, 30.

3. Gustavo Gutiérrez, *A Theology of Liberation* (Maryknoll, N.Y.: Orbis Books, 1988), xxxvi–vii.

4. Jon Sobrino, *Christology at the Crossroads* (Maryknoll, N.Y.: Orbis Books, 1980), xvi.

5. Ibid., xvii.

6. Leonardo Boff, *Jesus Christ Liberator* (Maryknoll, N.Y.: Orbis Books, 1981), p. 39.

7. Ibid., p. 279.

8. Ibid., p. 280.

9. Jon Sobrino, *Christology at the Crossroads*, p. 9.

10. Ignacio Ellacuría, *Freedom Made Flesh* (Maryknoll, N.Y.: Orbis Books, 1976), p. 23.

11. José Míguez Bonino, *Doing Theology in a Revolutionary Situation* (Philadelphia, 1975), p. 138.

12. Pierre Bigo, *The Church and Third World Revolution* (New York, 1977), p. 131.

13. Gustavo Gutiérrez, *A Theology of Liberation*, p. 72.

14. M. Echegoyen, "Priests and Socialism in Chile," *New Blackfriars* 52 (1971): p. 464f.

15. J. Davies, *Christian Politics and Violent Revolution* (New York, 1976).

16. Gustavo Gutiérrez, *A Theology of Liberation*.

17. Shabb, 119b.

18. Agadoth Shir Hashirim, pp. 18, 61.

19. Pirke Rabbi Eliezer, Ch. 3.

20. Agadoth Shir Hashirim, pp. 18, 61.

21. Gustavo Gutiérrez, *A Theology of Liberation*, p. 159.

22. Elsa Tamez, *Bible of the Oppressed* (Maryknoll, N.Y.: Orbis Books, 1982).

23. J. Severino Croatto, *Exodus* (Maryknoll, N.Y.: Orbis Books, 1981), p. 14.

24. Ibid., p. 15.

25. Enrique Dussel, *History and Theology of Liberation* (Maryknoll, N.Y.: Orbis Books, 1976).

26. Enrique Dussel, *History and Theology of Liberation*, p. 3.

27. Ibid., p. 7.

28. Louis Finkelstein, *Haggadah of Passover* (New York, 1942), p. i.

29. Franz Rosenzweig, *The Star of Redemption*, transl. N. Glatzer in *Franz Rosenzweig: His Life and Thought* (New York, 1953), pp. 319–21.

30. Ibid.

31. Moritz Lazarus, *The Ethics of Judaism* (Philadelphia, 1900), pp. 28–29.

32. Kaufmann Kohler, *Jewish Theology* (New York, 1918), p. 462.

33. Morris Joseph, *Judaism as Life and Creed* (London, 1903), pp. 213–15.

34. Ahad Ha-Am, *Essays, Letters, Memoirs* (Oxford, 1946), pp. 103–108.

35. Gustavo Gutiérrez, "Liberation Praxis and Christian Faith," in *Frontiers of Theology in Latin America*, ed. R. Gibellini (London, 1975), p. 14.

36. A. Cussianovich, *Religious Life of the Poor* (New York, 1979), p. 139.

37. Gustavo Gutiérrez, *Theology of Liberation*, p. 84.

38. Ibid., pp. 36–37.

39. The Union Haggadah (U.S.A., 1923), p. 78.

40. Lee Cormie, "Liberation and Salvation," in *The Challenge of Liberation Theology* (Maryknoll, N.Y.: Orbis Books, 1981), p. 29.

41. Ibid., p. 33.

42. Dorothee Sölle, "Liberation in a Consumerist Society," in *The Challenge of Liberation Theology*, p. 9.

43. Lee Cormie, "Liberation and Salvation," p. 33.

44. John Vincent, *Into the City* (London, 1982), p. 17.

45. Gustavo Gutiérrez, *The Power of the Poor in History* (Maryknoll, N.Y.: Orbis Books, 1983), p. 134.

46. C. Handy, "The Future of Work," *Christian* 8, no. 2 (1983): pp. 24–25.

47. Rosemary Radford Ruether, *Sexism and God Talk* (London, 1983), p. 178.

48. S. Schneider, *Jewish and Female* (New York, 1984), p. 19.

49. Rosemary Radford Ruether, *Sexism and God Talk*, pp. 87-92.

50. Helder Camara, *The Desert Is Fertile* (Maryknoll, N.Y.: Orbis Books, 1974), p. 16.

51. *Singers Praybook*, p. 239.

3

Theology of Islamic Liberation

MUHAMMAD MASHUQ IBN ALLY

INTRODUCTION

In recent years Islamic liberation, although still in the initial phases of articulation, has begun to influence the ideological dialogue of our times. An old and neglected issue has moved to the centre of the debate: the relevance of God and God's guidance to the sociopolitical life of humanity.

The contemporary Muslim world is passing through one of the most critical and creative periods of its history. Despite political freedom and economic resilience the pattern of life imposed upon Muslims during the period of colonial rule and strengthened in more subtle ways during the post-colonial era has remained fundamentally unchanged. The present-day upsurge in the Muslim world is an expression of the Muslim people's disillusionment with the politicoeconomic system imposed upon them either under foreign rule, or through the continuing influence of the indigenous Westernized elite (who are mostly alienated from their own people and their traditions, and whose interests converge with the interests of the dominant elite of the West).

Islamic liberation symbolizes the failure of the major contemporary models—chief among which are secular democracy, territorial or linguistic nationalism, individualistic capitalism, and totalitarian socialism—to take root in Muslim society and capture the imagination of the Muslim people. That is why all efforts to introduce a secular system in the Muslim lands have taken place under the protective umbrella of despotic rule. "Islamic Revolution," symbolizing a holistic move towards a new civilization, is the target of the *ummah*'s (universal community) date with destiny, whether it be in the Middle East, the Southeast Asian subcontinent, the Pacific basin, or elsewhere.

Much of this new-found spirit has been nurtured by two contemporary

Islamic movements, al-Ikhawan al-Muslimin and the Jama'ati-Islami, founded by Hasan al-Banna (1906–49) and Syed Abul-A'la al-Maududi (1903–79) respectively. The Ikhwan was established in 1928 in Egypt. The Jama't was established in 1940 in India; after partition in 1947, it moved its headquarters to Pakistan. Though both movements developed independently of each other, their aims, objectives and theology are quite similar. Their new confidence and vitality excited the emergence of similar movements across the world, and these two movements became the catalyst for a new intellectual and sociopolitical ideology. They both were to sponsor two important factors for change: (1) the unconditional and uncompromising advocacy of the Qur'an and *sunnah*, as a source of enlightenment and guidance for providing the *ummah* with a framework within which it could evolve suitably so as to be able progressively to reflect the Islamic ideal; and (2) the reclaiming of the individual by so reforming his or her personal life in virtues which reflect the values of Islam as a universal religion of humanity. From these two factors it is believed that the realization of the sovereignty of God can once again be established, and consequently an Islamic state and *khilafah* can be realized.

Islamic liberation must not simply be treated as an angry outburst against the West. It represents a rebellion against imposed heterogeneous, political, economic, and cultural models, and more fundamentally it reflects the Muslim people's search for a new order which ensures justice for all human beings in seeking the ideological fulfillment of the *ummah*. This quest for their destiny has made them more conscious of their ideological and historical identity and has brought them back to their original source — Islam. They are today grappling with the onerous task of rediscovering Islam's relevance to present-day problems, and of formulating its answers to the challenges of the modern age. In spite of all the tensions and travails which characterize the contemporary Muslim scene, the *ummah* is engaged in producing a creative response to a multifaceted challenge: the establishment of a new social order based on the ideals and values of Islam. Therefore liberation is not confined to political activism or cultural regeneration; at a deeper level there is a new awakening of Muslim thought and a revivification of the entire Muslim ethos.

This chapter draws on both of the above mentioned *sunni* movements to focus on the theological foundations of Islamic liberation (thus the revolution in Iran, which is peculiarly *shi'i,* is not taken into account). It also attempts to highlight any convergence with Christian liberation theology.

THEOLOGICAL FORMULATIONS

Contemporary civilization is based on the principle of separation of religion and state in which the human being is assumed to be self-sufficient. As such, the social, economic, political, and technological questions of human civilization are treated without any reference to God and divine guidance:

God is to be worshipped in one's personal life only. In addition, the affairs of society and the economy are to be conducted according to the individual's own discretion and sovereign wisdom. The conquest of nature becomes the main target of human effort, and the stream of civilization is allowed to run its course without reference to the values and principles communicated to humanity by God through the prophets.

The Muslim world is no exception to this state of affairs. The models of politics, society, and economics, developed over the last one hundred years or so, are steeped in the traditions of secularism. The last four decades have witnessed the emergence of over forty-three Muslim states, yet the sociopolitical systems obtaining in these countries continue to be based on Western models. This is the contradiction which Islamic liberation movements have tried to challenge. For many Muslims this means attempting to reconstruct society by drawing primarily upon its own rich but neglected religiocultural sources. The ultimate objective of this exercise is to establish a just social order in which the material and the spiritual aspects are welded together so that "progress" and "prayer" do not represent two watertight compartments, but two sides of the same coin, with prayer acting as a stepping stone to human progress and progress leading to the glorification of the Creator.

Muslims[1] claim that Islam[2] is a complete way of life and the divergence between the values and principles of Islam and the secular social reality lie at the root of the tension that permeates the Muslim world today. Islamic liberation represents a new approach — that is, one of striving to reconstruct society in accordance with the Islamic ideals and values and the needs of contemporary life. In this respect Muslim liberationists share a common cause with their contemporary counterparts in Christianity. "The kingdom of God that Christ announces is not a liberation from this or that evil, from political oppression of the Romans, from sin alone. The Kingdom of God cannot be narrowed down to any particular aspect. It embraces all: the world, the human person, and society; the totality of reality is to be transformed by God."[3]

This convergence of vision between the three faiths, Islam, Christianity, and Judaism, is the result of common recognition that the inward and outward response to reality is the essence of the religious experience that acknowledges that there is no god but one God; that God is the source of all creation; and that all humans are equal as creatures of God, endowed with the same essential qualities of creaturely humanity, with the same cosmic status: an affirmation of a *religio naturalis*. The Qur'an commands all humans to belong to it: "Turn your face to the primordial religion, the religion in which God created all humans. That is the immutable pattern of God."[4] "Only those with knowledge will reason out and understand it."[5]

Within this paradigm, Islam claims that the content of natural religion is absolutely normative for all humans and its raison d'être is the recognition that Ultimate Reality is indeed God: no one else is God. The rest of the content revolves around the creature's creatureliness vis-à-vis the Creator, a relationship which can be none other than worship and service. In addition, the identity of God, the source of revelation in the three religions, necessarily leads to one identity of the revelations and of the religions. Therefore, Islam does not see itself as coming to the religious scene ex nihilo, but as reaffirming the same truth presented by all the preceding prophets: all are regarded as Muslims, and their revelations as the same as its own. Under this principle, the three faiths constitute a crystallization of one and the same religious consciousness whose essence and core is identical. This unity of religious consciousness consists of five dominant principles: (1) God is separate from God's creatures; (2) humanity has been created for unconditional service to God on earth; (3) the relationship between Creator and creature, or the will of God, is the content of revelation and is expressed in terms of law and ethical imperatives; (4) the human being, the servant, is the trustee of creation under the sovereignty of God, capable of transforming it within the framework of the divine will; (5) humankind's obedience to, and fulfillment of, the divine command results in happiness and thus unites worldly and cosmic justice. This visionary paradigm in the unity of religious and cultural consciousness enables the assembly of a formidable force to spearhead a new world order, where the consensus is *salam* — peace.

All religious liberationists agree that the prerequisites for there to be peace, are justice, balance, and freedom, and in their use, the mechanisms of responsibility and reckoning are provided by the ethical and legal imperatives. "Democracy, freedom, moral uprightness, science, and culture: these are the goals that the new religion is supposed to serve."[6] "Sin — a breach of friendship with God and others — is according to the Bible the ultimate cause of poverty, injustice, and the oppression in which men live."[7] "When the path ordained by God is that which rules human life, this defect disappears, and true, complete and comprehensive justice is obtained, that justice which cannot be reached by any human, man-made system. There is nothing in any man-made system which will free it of the factors of human desire, human weakness and attachment to self-interest in one form or the other."[8]

At the core of Islamic liberation is *allah* (God), *al-khaliq* (the Creator), *al-razzaq* (the Sustainer), and *al-malik* (the Sovereign) of all creation.[9] God is the central pivot, free from uncertain equivocations: the God that is *wahid* (One), the Provident, active in history but separated from it by an infinite gulf, the Judge of a person's actions, the Judge as to who is a Muslim and who is not. For the Muslim, God is the source of all creation, and because God has power over life and death, God is the source of absolute authority: "To Him is due the primal origin of the heavens and the earth: When He designs a matter, and says to it 'BE,' it is."[10] Islam experiences God not merely as an absolute, ultimate, first-cause principle, but as a core of normativeness. This means not only that God is the source of all creation, but that God's power (*qadr*) and authority (*amr*) are manifest throughout creation. Therefore, God is the cause of orderliness, and thus the cosmos is indeed a cosmos, not a chaos, precisely because God implemented in it God's eternal patterns. The outcome of God's creativeness, God's power and authority, compels the Muslim to accept God's *mulk* — sovereignty. This results in the elimination of any power in nature besides God. "Knowest you not that God is Sovereign over the heavens and the earth."[11] This does not meant that God's power is remote; as the *malik* (Sovereign), God supports and sustains creation; God protects and loves creation; God's sovereignty is a sovereignty of beneficence and compassion, or mercy and peace — *rahman* and *rahim*. God's dominion is the dominion of "peace" to which all humanity is called: "God does call to House of Peace."[12]

We find this echoed in Old Testament literature:

The Biblical God is close to man; he is a God of communion with and commitment to man. The active presence of God in the midst of his people is part of the oldest and most enduring Biblical promises. In connection with the first Covenant, God said: "I shall dwell in the midst of the Israelites, I shall become their God, and by dwelling among them they will know that I am their Lord their God who brought them out of Egypt. I am the Lord their God" (Exod. 29:45–46). And in the proclamation of the new Covenant, God said: "They shall live under the shelter of my dwelling; I will become their God, and they shall become my people. The nations shall know that I the Lord am keeping Israel, sacred to myself, because my sanctuary is in the midst of them forever" (Ezek. 37:27–28).[13]

Within this framework, the liberationist contends that all that surrounds creation, things or events, all that takes place in the natural, social or physical fields, is the action of God, the discharge of God's causal efficacy and ontic power, the fulfillment of one or another of God's purposes. This does not mean that God is directly and personally the cause of all, nor does it mean that God, rather than human beings, is responsible for all human actions. Rather, the moral worth of an action is solely an individual responsibility. The ontological power which diffuses being and nonbeing is God's alone to have and to exercise. "The kingdom of God, contrary to what many Christians think, does not signify something that is purely spiritual or outside this world. It is the totality of this material world, spiritual and human, that is now introduced into God's order."[14] "The entire universe is under the authority of God, and man, being a small part of it, necessarily obeys the physical laws governing the universe."[15]

As a religious culture, then, Islam is the experience of the Ultimate Reality: the sovereign Lord and that Lord's demand upon humankind, the concept known as *tawhid* (unicity), which signifies a relationship with the Only One to the exclusion of a similar relationship with anyone else. *Tawhid* is a key concept in Islam, and it is the cornerstone of its liberation move-ment's theology. It is the one term that describes the process of the Islamic transformation of an individual or a society. In human history it presents the crux of the prophetic mission, serving at the basis of all revealed relig-ions. Muslim liberationists see the lapse of *tawhid* to be the loss of political power, the source of economic backwardness, intellectual stagnation, and social degeneration, underpinned by a low level of spiritual commitment:

> Islam cannot fulfill its role except by taking concrete form in a society, rather, in a nation; for man does not listen, especially in this age, to an abstract theory which is not seen materialized in a living society. From this point of view, we can say that the Muslim community has been extinct for a few centuries, for this Muslim community does not denote the name of a land in which Islam resides, nor is it a people whose forefathers lived under the Islamic system at some earlier time. It is the name of a group of people whose manners, ideas and con-cepts, rules and regulations, values and criteria, are all derived from Islamic sources. The Muslim community with these characteristics vanished at the moment the laws of God became suspended on earth.[16]

The concept of *tawhid* excludes the human being's commitment to any-one other than God, and the rejection of all sources of value other than the will of God, and all authority except God's. In the human context, it is interpreted to mean emancipation and restoration of the human being's essential freedom from all human bondage. The person is bound to no other human being or group of people, or to their mores and manners, customs and traditions, social institutions, laws, modes of thought, views and presumptions, theories and philosophies. The world of nature is the creation of God for the free use of humans; it is to be neither feared nor revered. The human being must be fully conscious of this essential freedom and independence before that person can enter into the relationship with God required of that individual's nature and consciousness. If this con-sciousness of independence and freedom is lacking, genuine *tawhid* is impossible, and if it is deficient and vague, the relationship with God will be impure, weak and largely ineffective.

From the point of view of the liberationist, *tawhid* gives humans the sense of being equal as well as free. The moment individuals regard them-selves as essentially inferior to another human being they lose this freedom and find themselves in bondage to whomever they recognize as superior. This is particularly true of individuals who claim exclusive access to knowl-edge of things divine — groups and nations who claim exclusivity on account of their power, wealth, language, or color of skin. Complementing the proc-ess of liberation is the restoration of the essential human characteristic of a person — thinking for oneself and making one's own decisions. It is only liberated persons who think and make their own choices and can warmly respond to the prophetic call. "Lo! herein indeed are portents for those who reflect . . . for men of knowledge . . . for those who understand."[17]

But it is not sufficient only to be free and independent of others. Liberationists also expect that one should be on guard against oneself, especially in the realm of one's own values as they relate to others, in order not to succumb to the transient, the narrow-minded, and the short-sighted in what one seeks. This is so whether it be pleasure, pursuit of power and wealth, or confined to the narrow interests of kith and kin. In the words of one Christian liberationist, "The preaching of Jesus about the kingdom of God concerns not only persons, demanding conversion of them. It also affects the world of persons in terms of a liberation from legalism, from conventions without foundation, from authoritarianism and the forces and powers that subject people."[18] *Tawhid* as a liberating concept is best illustrated by Mughirah b. Shu'bah who stood before Rustam, the Persian general, and explained that Islam meant "to emancipate people from the obedience of men to the obedience of Allah."[19]

As a consequence of *tawhid*, the human being enters into a relationship with God that involves a particular relationship with the universe. Islamic liberation seeks to raise the pure consciousness of persons to realize that they are the *khalifah* (trustees) of God, carrying a divine responsibility — *taklif.*

> God has put us to serious trial on two counts: (a) He has left man free but even after giving him that freedom He wishes to see whether or not man realizes his true position; whether he remains honest and steadfast and maintains loyalty and allegiance to the Lord, or loses his head and revolts against his own Creator; whether he behaves like a noble soul, or tramples underfoot all values of decency and starts playing such fantastic tricks as make the angels weep; (b) He wants to see whether man is prepared to have such confidence in God as to offer his life and wealth in return for what is a promise, that is to materialize in the next world — and whether he is prepared to surrender his autonomy and all the charms that go with it, in exchange for a promise about the future.[20]

Khilafah (trusteeship) is the essence of being human, for the conferring of this status to all humans means the restoration of human dignity that has been the central challenge before all revealed religions.

> Consequently, when we assert that man fulfills himself by continuing the work of creation by means of his labor, we are saying that he places himself, by this very fact, within an all-embracing salvific process. To work, to transform this world, is to become a man and to build the human community; it is also to save. Likewise, to struggle against

misery and exploitation and to build a just society is already to be part of the saving action, which is moving toward its complete fulfillment. All this means that building the temporal city is not simply a stage of "humanization" or "pre-evangelization" as was held in theology up until a few years ago. Rather it is to become part of a saving process which embraces the whole of man and all human history. Any theological reflection on human work and social praxis ought to be rooted in this fundamental affirmation.[21]

The role of divine guidance in human life is to remind individuals of the ways that suit their own character and the world of nature. For Islamic liberation movements, *tawhid* has always been the essence of such guidance.

The will of God revealed to human beings gives them the vision of a society engaged in the pursuit of value, or humans living a healthy, well-provisioned, good life in cooperation with others. That vision inspires one to an ethic of action, for God has invested the human being with divine trust that is the fulfillment of the ethical part of the divine will. By virtue of the powers delegated to human beings by God, the human person is required to exercise this authority within the limits prescribed by God. This mission belongs to this world and calls for a course of action in this life. It is born simultaneously with and is an integral part of the commitment to God. It is intended to create a positive attitude towards the world of nature. As soon as individuals similarly committed and inspired come into existence, they become the *jama'h* (movement) that has a mission with humanity. The challenge before a prophet is to establish this *jama'h* through the articulation of *tawhid* and lead it to the successful performance of its mission. The whole process of liberation, restoration of human nobility, the resurrection of reason and independent judgment, the acceptance of revealed guidance, and the transformation of individuals and social life, is a movement directed at raising an *ummah*. The Islamic state is the product of this movement as well as an instrument in its further expansion until it embraces all humanity. From the very outset, it is a dynamic movement, and its dynamism continues to increase with changing circumstances and expansion into new lands, new peoples and new generations.

The mission of the *jama'h* is embodied in the following two Qur'an verses: "You are the best community that hath been raised up for mankind. You enjoin right conduct and forbid indecency; and you believe in Allah."[22] "And thus We have made you a balanced community that you may be the bearers of witness to the people and [that] the Apostle may be a bearer of witness to you."[23] It is noteworthy that the crucial terms *ma'ruf* (right conduct) and *munkar* (indecency) used in the first verse are basically human in content, and that which is defined in the Qur'an as good and bad is indeed so for the Muslim. But liberationists claim that the value-oriented intellect of the human being is capable of extending this principle to new situations that may arise.

However, it is the concern of Islamic liberation to undertake a *tajdid* (revival) of this ethical imperative, because it sees it as the *taklif* (divine responsibility) implicit in the *khilafah* (trusteeship) of the *ummah* (universal community). The source from which Muslim liberationists seek knowledge (*'ilm*) of God and guidance (*hidayah*) for human behavior is the *sunnah* (the way of the prophets), and the Qur'an, the mainstay of liberation, the book (*al-kitab*), the revealed word (*wahy*) of God to humanity, the direct and immediate disclosure of what God wants to be realized on earth. They see it not merely as an ethical source, but as a cognitive category in that it has to do with epistemology and with the truthfulness of its propositions. As an epistemological principle, it is a counsel of despair, resting on the a priori assumption that human beings find it difficult to distinguish between reality and unreality. Therefore it is a grounding for a rational interpretation of the universe within which the tawhidic principle lays everything open to inspection and criticism, protecting against simple contradiction on one hand and paradox on the other, minimizing the possibility of literalism, fanaticism, and stagnation.

Within this framework Islamic liberationists do not perceive the Qur'an as an inventory of good and evil; rather, the Qur'an lays down a framework of life the aim of which is to insure that evil does not destroy human life. The Qur'an draws on allegory and history to encourage, exhort, and inspire the Muslim to an ethic of action. Vices, if left unchecked, lead to evil (*munkarat*); virtues, when allowed to flourish, lead to goodness (*mar'ufat*). The former will lead to destabilization, giving way to chaos and injustice, and disturbing the natural order of things. The latter gives way to order, equilibrium (*wasat*), and justice (*'adl*). It is this moral responsibility, in service and obedience to God, striving for and upholding God's sovereignty, struggling for what is right, good and just to maintain equilibrium and order, which are the ethical parts of liberation. The responsibility or obligation (*taklif*) laid down upon the human being knows no bounds as far as his or her scope and theatre of action is concerned; it comprehends the whole universe. All humanity is the object of moral action: for the Muslim liberationist, *taklif* is universal and cosmic.

This concept of a person's place in the universe is underpinned by the Islamic understanding of that pure nature innate in every person which enables humankind to extract itself out of any predicament. The Qur'an teaches that God, out of divine love and mercy, created human beings with senses, reason, and understanding, and breathed God's spirit (*ruh*) into them. This innate purity of all humans is permanent; therefore no human person is in need of salvation—Islam has no soteriology. It entertains no idea of the fall of human beings, no concept of original sin. Every person is born innocent, yet born with the faculties of understanding and an innate sense with which to know the ultimate reality. Adam committed a misdeed; but he repented and was forgiven: "Adam received a revelation from his Lord and repented. God accepted his repentance, for He is the Merciful

Forgiver."[24] His disobedience was a human error; it was the first ethical misjudgment. But it was the action of one man, and has no effect on anyone else. It constituted no fall. The entire universe is Muslim, because it is in a state of submission to the natural laws ordained by God. The prophet Muhammad declared that the whole world is a *masjid* (*Bukhari hadith*) — the *masjid* being a place of *sujud* (prostration). Human beings are unique insofar as they have been endowed with free will and with moral discernment. Therefore, they can choose to obey or disobey God. Herein lies, for Islam, the source of human success or failure. Rather than the fall, Islam asserts innocence; rather than salvation, felicity. Religious felicity (*falah*), consists of a person's effort to meet the divine imperative. The degree by which the Muslim is able to fulfill the divine trust is what is to be accounted for on the day of judgment.

From the point of view of the liberationist, this is the justification for moral action:

> This means that the world and the Hereafter are not two separate things but a continuous process whose beginning is the world and the end, hereafter. The relation between the two is the same as between cultivation and crop. You plough the land, then sow the seeds, then irrigate, then look after the field till such time as the crop is ready. Then after reaping it you feed yourself with it comfortably throughout the year. You will naturally reap whatever you have cultivated in the land. If you sow wheat, only wheat will grow. If thorns are sown, only thorns will grow. If nothing is sown, nothing will grow ... This is exactly the position in respect of this world and the hereafter.[25]

> The idea of a universal salvation, which was accepted only with great difficulty and was based on the desire to expand the possibilities of achieving salvation, leads to the question of the presence of the Lord and therefore of the religious significance of man's action in history. One looks then to this world, and now sees in the world beyond not the "true life," but rather the transformation and fulfillment of the present life.[26]

Islamic eschatology countenances only one kingdom, one space-time; what is earned by means of God-consciousness (*taqwa*) is a transcendent reward, not an exchange for a better kingdom: "And seek the other world in that which God bestows upon you in this world. Do not therefore forsake your share of this world. Do good to others as God has done good to you. Do not seek corruption, or allow it to happen to earth. God does not love corrupters."[27]

PROPHETIC FOUNDATIONS

The vision of Islamic liberation finds expression in the prophetic mission (*risalah*), the concretization of the vision, or the materialization of the ideal in space-time, the translation of theory into reality. In it the values of Islam were given form and have become alive; the prophets were true exemplars of liberation, a universal messianic phenomenon:

> These prophets were raised in all epochs, in all lands and in all nations. Their number exceeds many thousands. All of them brought the same message, all advocated the same way of life (*Deen*) i.e., the way which was revealed to man on the first day of his existence. All of them followed the same guidance: the guidance which was prescribed by the Lord for man at the outset of his career on the earth. All of them stood for the same mission: they called men to the religion of Islam, asked those who accepted the Divine Guidance to live in accordance with that and organized them into a movement for the establishment of the Divine Law, and for putting an end to all deviations from the Right Path. Every prophet tried to fulfill this mission in the best possible way. But quite a number of people never accepted their guidance and many of those who accepted it, gradually drifted astray and after a lapse of time, lost the guidance or distorted it through innovations and perversions.[28]

Within the framework of the tawhidic principle, prophecy and the messages of prophets have but one essence — acknowledgement that God is one, that all worship and service is due to God alone. Doing of good and liberating humanity from bondage are the essence of the mission. Each prophet internalized and externalized the message and became its exemplar; thus, prophets form a common fraternity appointed by God. "O you Apostles! enjoy all things good and pure, and work righteousness; For I am well-acquainted with all that you do. And verily this Brotherhood of yours is a single Brotherhood, and I am your Lord and Cherisher: therefore fear Me (and no other)."[29]

This unity of prophethood enables Muslims to regard the liberation movements in other faiths as sharing in a common heritage, although each revelation and liberation has come in a code of behavior particularly applicable to its people. Thus the essence of the religious experience of the Hebrews and of their descendants the Jews has remained the same since the patriarchal age. It contained the Abrahamic vision with its transcendence and universalist ethics, but maintained its ethnocentric particularism. The essence of religious experience as Jesus taught it was that salvation is a state of consciousness dominated by faith in God almighty and merciful, attuned with God's will through purity, self-denial, and charity. Jesus' reform was directed equally to those Jews who observed the ethic of materialism and cynicism in imitation of their Greek and Roman teachers, and to the whole of classical antiquity.

The desire for prophecy results from human forgetfulness, disobedience, and deviation, because revelation always advocates ethical and moral imperatives to which humankind does not always acquiesce. Leaders who seek to have their own way may rebel against the social ethic of the reve- lation: Human beings are vain, and inclined to indulgence. Revelation, when not remembered, taught, and observed publicly, tends to be forgotten. All these factors contribute to a loss of faith (*iman*), consciousness, and responsibility to the Ultimate Reality.

It is the reawakening of this God-consciousness (*taqwa*) that is the essen- tial task of the prophets, and the loss of it is the cause of *zulm* (oppression and injustice) and *fasad* (corruption and disorder). This dynamic constitutes a dialectic between the all-embracing relationship between worship of the ever-living God and the sociopolitical situation of the time. From this per- spective, new axiological relations obtain between various values; old anti- monies may be solved and new ones discovered; new values may be established that could have never been consciousnessly formed by an indi- vidual. Therefore, prophecy is seen by liberationists as a civilizational[30] continuum. Each prophet who disturbs the flow of space-time enters the rough and tumble of the market place and history, contributes to its recast- ing, and gives it a new character as constitutive of that civilization. The prophet's mission is not simply confined to inviting humanity to worship God or verbally condemning social injustices; it is, in addition, a struggle to establish a new world order where peace and justice prevail. "Indeed We sent down with them the Book and the Balance, so that men may establish justice."[31]

The Prophets announce a kingdom of peace. But peace presupposes the establishment of justice: "Righteousness shall yield peace and its fruit (shall) be quietness and confidence forever" (Isa. 32:17; cf. also Ps. 85). It presupposes the defence of the rights of the poor, punish- ment of oppression, a life free from the fear of being enslaved by others, and the liberation of the oppressed. Peace, justice, love, and freedom are not private realities or internal attitudes. They are social realities, implying a historical liberation.[32]

Moses is seen by Islamic liberationists as the liberator par excellence. He demanded from Pharaoh the deliverance of the Children of Israel from oppression. "I come to you from your Lord with a clear sign. So let the children of Israel depart with me."[33] "Pharaoh acted haughtily on earth and split his people into factions, seeking to weaken a group of them. He slaugh- tered their sons and let their women live; he was so depraved."[34] *Salih* was sent to liberate his people, *Thamud,* of their materialism: "In the land: you build for yourselves palaces and castles in open plains, and carve out homes in the mountains, so remember your Lord and refrain from tyranny."[35] Lot was responsible for liberating his people from their sexual enslavement: "We sent Lot: he said to his people, 'Do you commit lewdness such as no people in creation ever committed before you? for you practice your lusts

on men in preference to women: you are transgressors.' "[36] Liberating the
Madyan people from economic corruption was the mission of *Shu'ayb:* "O
my people! worship God; you have no other god but Him. I have come with
a clear sign from your Lord! Give just measure and weight, nor withhold
from people the things that are their due; and do not corruption on the
earth after it has been set in order: that will be best for you, if you are of
faith."[37]

A prophet, himself a human being, is the first to accept revelation and
to put it into practice, thereby setting an example (*sunnah*) for others to
emulate. His function is to convey the divine message in his own language.
"We have sent no messenger except to convey the message in the tongue
of his own people, to make the content clearly comprehensible to them."[38]
In other words, to explain and elaborate (exegesis), and to initiate those
processes — *tazkiyyah* (purification) and *tarbiyyah* (education and development) — in the lives of individuals and society through which the ideals and
principles can be implemented. Islamic liberationists see the various strat-
egies and tactics of prophets as a constellation of divinely sanctioned meth-
odologies from which generations can benefit.

The prophetic mission culminated with the call of Muhammad to be a
prophet. His audience was the common person of humanity, including those
followers of earlier prophets who had gone astray. His mission was to invite
them to the right path and to build them into a universal community
(*ummah*) that would not only organize its own way of life in accordance
with Divine Order but also establish that Order for the whole world. Since
belief in Muhammad as the final prophet to humanity and the bearer of
the final revelation from God is one of the essential convictions of a Muslim,
Islamic liberationists perceive his model to be the final blueprint of liberation.

> The mission of Muhammad was a revolution against the tyranny of
> *shirk* (polytheism). In this sphere of doctrine it perceived God as
> Perfect, beyond similarity and above partnership. The tyranny of pol-
> ytheism is one that has deep roots in the human spirit. Despite the
> many Prophets, the messages and the works of the scholars expound-
> ing monotheism, humanity still suffers from polytheism. The mission
> of Muhammad was also a revolution against the tyranny of fanaticism:
> fanaticism in all its manifestations, above all, religious fanaticism. The
> mission of Muhammad was a revolution against the tyranny of race
> prejudice and color prejudice.[39]

Within the Muslim self-understanding, this prophetic model is not only
the realization of the ideal; it also inaugurates a process through which
those who have followed in the footsteps of Muhammad throughout the
ages have continued to strive to understand, interpret, explain, and imple-
ment the word of God. The prophet Muhammad was not only the recipient

of the divine revelation contained in the Qur'an; he was also its most authentic interpreter and expounder. The *sunnah* represents the Qur'an in practice. It embodies and radiates the model in both time and space. The *sunnah* is a collection of the prophet's sayings and deeds. It includes his opinions about matters good or evil, desirable or otherwise, as well as practices of which he approved as suitable for Muslims to follow. The *sunnah* occupies a place second to the Qur'an. Its function is to clarify the Qur'an's pronouncements, to exemplify and illustrate its purposes. Where the Qur'anic statement is general, the *sunnah* particularizes it to make it applicable; and where particular, the *sunnah* generalizes it in order to make possible its extrapolation to other particulars. All Muslims universally recognize the value of the *sunnah*, its relevance to Islam, and their need for it to help them fulfill the requirements of their faith in liturgical, legal, ethical, social, economic, political, and international affairs. That is why the *sunnah* came to be regarded, from the beginning of the prophet's mission, as a second authoritative source of Islam, and in addition, for the liberation movements, a methodological source.

POST-PROPHETIC ERA

Islamic liberationists see history as a perpetual struggle between Islam (peace out of commitment to one God), and *jahiliyyah* (world views and systems which deny God's sovereignty and the authority of divine guidance). For them, liberation operates at two levels, the first through prophets, the messengers of God, and the second by those inspired by revelation and prophets to continue the mission and cause through time. Therefore, liberation is not an isolated phenomenon, a haphazard occurrence; liberation is seen to have a historical heritage. It represents a continuation of the mission of the prophets. It constitutes the proclamation appointing those who struggle for *'adl* (justice), *wasat* (balance), *ma'rufat* (goodness), *haq* (truth), and *salam* (peace) to be *shuhada* (witnesses) in the world, and, more importantly, to share in and continue the prophetic mission that ceased with the death of the prophet Muhammad. This role now becomes the mission of the *ummah* (universal community): "You are an appointed community to be of the middle way, that you might be witness over the nations, as the messenger is a witness over you."[40] This messianic role is revolutionary inasmuch as it seeks to inaugurate a total revolution in human life aimed at fashioning that life according to divine values. This means bringing about a catalytic process that will result in conversion—a whole series of changes in the life of individuals intended to develop a community of faith. The community grows as a *jama'h* (movement), engaged in bringing about social change in the desired direction. This effort aims at the building of a new society and state and at the establishment of a new order, characterized by *khilafah 'ala minhaj al-nubuwwah*, *khalifate* on the prophetic pattern that serves as the realization of the Kingdom of God. This task is required, because "it is necessary to revive that Muslim community which is buried under the debris of the man-made traditions of several generations, and which is crushed under the weight of those false laws and customs which are not even remotely related to the Islamic teachings, and which, in spite of all this, calls itself the 'world of Islam.' "[41] Although Islamic liberationists use the term "revolution," it should not be equated with violent struggles. The idea that a change for the better can be brought about by an alteration in the socioeconomic or in political environment or in the material and social fabric of life is considered an illusion. Most of the movements disapprove of revolutions that resort to hatred, violence, and force, although on some occasions, they have resorted to violence as a self-defence mechanism. Islamic revolution seeks a much more profound alteration, the transformation of the human individual who is to serve as the resource for the new order.

The general methodology for change adopted by the liberation movements is preceded by an analysis of the prevailing situation in relation to conflict between Islam and *jahiliyyah* in a given place and time. What is required is a clear and straightforward appraisal of the forms of *jahiliyyah* in society, the sources which nourish it and the sensitive points on which it conflicts with Islam. In addition, the sources of weakness in contemporary Muslim life must be diagnosed, so that the major ailments from which Muslim society suffers at a given period of history can be identified. The object of this intellectual effort is to formulate an appropriate strategy to ensure that Islamic principles become operative in the lives of the Muslims. For the preparation of a realistic strategy it is essential to examine the resources available at a given period of time; therefore, liberation movements are concerned to carry out a full assessment of the mental, moral, and material resources on which it can expect to draw.[42]

The framework for change draws on the prophetic methodology which is to articulate the ideals and principles of Islam in a language understandable to the people of the age. This requires that an intellectual effort be made to study carefully, analyze and criticize new terminologies. The moral fibre of the life of the people should be rebuilt so as to develop a true Islamic character; social habits, customs, education, socioeconomic institutions, and political power are all subject to this effort. This requires an exercise in *ijtihad*, which means that the ideals and values of Islam have to be applied to the changed context. Thus there will have to be a distinction between the essential and the incidental elements found in the actual life of Muslims. *Ijtihad* represents the principle of movements within the system of Islam, and it involves creative thinking and action with a view to bringing the stream of life under the guidance of Islam. "To attain the leadership of mankind, we must have something to offer besides material progress, and this other quality can only be a faith and a way of life which on the one hand conserves the benefits of modern science and technology, and on the other fulfills the basic human needs on the same level of excellence as technology has fulfilled them in the sphere of material comfort. And then this faith and way of life must take concrete form in a human society—in other words, in a Muslim society."[43]

The personalities of those who practice liberation cannot be ignored because they serve as a major catalyst in a given place and time. Here Islamic liberationists do not perceive the movement as personality-centered. Religious authority resides in the Qur'an and *sunnah*. In this respect liberation is a social movement with a collective spiritual leadership that pilots the cause and controls the extremes of individuals. "Where on this broad surface of the earth will their spiritual leadership be recognized? The task of 'exalting the Word of God' requires a group of workers who are fearful of God and implicitly follow the law of God without consideration of gain or loss, no matter where they come from, whether from this community which is now called Muslim or from outside."[44] The term is generally used in a broad sense to include decision makers. Frequently it refers to the educated class who controls the organs of society that play an effective role in human life.

Liberation movements that have become operational within the Muslim world in contemporary society have identified three general factors responsible for the loss of Muslim witness in the world. The first was the change in the body politic of Islam from a *khilafah* to a more or less monarchical and presidential system. This led to very important changes affecting the role of religion in Muslim sociopolitical life, particularly in the bifurcation into political and religious leadership, each with its own separate domain. Consequently, ordinary persons in Muslim society are torn between following political rulers and following religious leaders who have been exalted to the position of unquestioned authority. The second change concerns the system of education imposed by colonial rule which separated education into the religious and the secular. Throughout this process, the uncritical Western educated elite has injected heterogenous ideas into the intellectual milieu of Muslim countries and fostered religious conservatism—*taqlid* (blind imitation)—among the masses in those places where Islam has been inherited via oral tradition rather than through choice and freedom of thought. As a result, the perpetuation of schisms and tensions have sapped the creativity and vitality of Islamic civilization in all the major realms of human effort. Third, the outcome of these changes has caused the moral life of the people to deteriorate; their faith and God-consciousness has weakened, and a dislocation between theory and practice has appeared. "The community which is at present known by the name of Muslim is a hybrid mixture of all sorts of people with hardly a common standard of behavior. From the point of view of moral conduct, you will find among Muslims as many varieties of character as are to be found among the nonbelievers."[45]

The contemporary programme of liberation is built on four pillars:
(1) the renewal of Islamic thought to meet the modern ideational chal-

lenge. This means drawing on the Qur'an and *sunnah* and, after that, the totality of experience propounded through the ages. Central to this scheme is a liberation of the mind: "They say: We follow that wherein we found our forefathers. What! Even though their forefathers were wholly unintelligent and had no guidance?"[46] Liberationists understand this verse to be the core of the liberating process: always keep in view the fallibility of everything human and the possibility of its being improved upon, and be ready to exercise one's own judgment.

(2) the reaching out to the persons who are disposed to righteousness and drawing them together into an organized body—*jama'h*. The *jama'h* is a moral entity that must transcend biological, geographical, political, linguistic and cultural links. This is not a movement-by-nature, but a movement-by-decision. The ideals that cement the interpersonal relationships of the *jama'h* are: *tahabub* (mutual loving), *tawasi* and *tanahi* (counseling), *ta'akhi* (brothering), *ta'awun* (co-operating), *ta'lim* (educating), *tazawuj* (mixing), *tasadduq* and *ta'annus* (befriending). As the *jama'h* multiplies, it matures into an *ummah*. It is only after a group of people which combines true Islamic vision and character with intellectual competence and skill and strives in a systematic manner that God will permit the Islamic order to be established.

(3) the striving to bring about societal change through individual conversion and collective effort in which the mosque—the community base—becomes the focus and locus of activity, education being the spearhead of human development. While the ultimate aim is to effect total change, progress toward this goal should be gradual and well calculated. Instead of revolting against every single item in a given society, there should be a careful analysis of what is malignant and needs to be changed and what is healthy and should be preserved.

(4) the development of a new cadre of leaders at the intellectual, social, and cultural levels. All the liberation movements agree at the moment that leadership change in a democratic order should take place through elections.

Islamic liberationists have expended most of their energies in working out this programme within the Muslim world. They have yet to attach a higher value to the emancipation and value orientation of all human beings, Muslims as well as non-Muslims. In a world that is fast becoming one unit, a total civilizational change in a country can hardly come about in isolation; therefore, some creativity is needed to address the interreligious challenge of liberation. A movement that focuses its attention on the religious liberation among Muslims only is likely to result not in emancipation, but in a preservationist policy hardly able to discriminate between the ends and the means, the higher values and the peripheral rules of conduct. The contemporary relevance of these measures to the process of *tawhid* is not difficult to discern. Should the contemporary Islamic liberation movements stand equal to the task before them, it will be of great significance.

NOTES

1. The Muslim is the person who is at peace out of commitment to one God, and who follows the prophetic path, and who holds Muhammad as the last and final prophet.

2. Islam means peace out of commitment to one God.

3. Leonardo Boff, *Jesus Christ Liberator: A Christology of Our Time* (Maryknoll, N.Y.: Orbis Books, 1978) p. 55.

4. Qur'an: 30;30.

5. Qur'an: 29;43.

6. J.M. Bonino, *Revolutionary Theology Comes of Age* (London: SPCK, 1975), p. 11.

7. Gustavo Gutiérrez, *A Theology of Liberation* (London: SCM Press, 1977; Maryknoll, N.Y.: Orbis Books, 1971; rev. ed. 1988), p. 35.

8. S. Qutb, *This Religion of Islam* (Kuwait: International Islamic Federation of Student Organizations, 1977), p. 19.

9. There are ninety-nine attributes of God, *asma' al-husna*, through which a Muslim recognizes God.

10. Qur'an: 2;117.

11. Qur'an: 2;107.

12. Qur'an: 10;25.

13. Gustavo Gutiérrez, *A Theology of Liberation*, p. 190.

14. Leonardo Boff, *Jesus Christ Liberator*, p. 56.

15. S. Qutb, *Milestones* (Kuwait: International Islamic Federation of Students Organizations, n.d.), p. 62.

16. Ibid., p. 10.

17. Qur'an: 30;21,22,24.

18. Leonardo Boff, *Jesus Christ Liberator*, p. 72.

19. ibn Kathir, *al-Bidayah wa al-Nihayah*, vol. 7 (Cairo: Sa'adah Press, n.d.), p. 39.

20. S.A.A. Maududi, *Islamic Way of Life* (Kuwait: ILFSO, 1977), pp. 10–11.

21. Gustavo Gutiérrez, *A Theology of Liberation*.

22. Qur'an: 3;111.

23. Qur'an: 2;143.

24. Qur'an: 2;27.

25. S.A.A. Maududi, *Fundamentals of Islam* (Lahore: Islamic Publications, 1975), pp. 42-43.

26. Gustavo Gutiérrez, *A Theology of Liberation*, p. 153.

27. Qur'an: 28;77.

28. S.A.A. Maududi, *Islamic Way of Life*, p. 6.

29. Qur'an: 23;51–52.

30. "When, in a society, the sovereignty belongs to God alone, expressed in its obedience to the Divine Law, only then is every person in that society free from servitude to others, and only then does he taste true freedom. This alone is 'human civilization,' as the basis of a human civilization is the complete and true freedom of every person and the full dignity of every individual of the society" (Qutb, *Milestones*, p. 140).

31. Qur'an: 57; 25.
32. Gustavo Gutiérrez, *A Theology of Liberation*, p. 167.
33. Qur'an: 7;105.
34. Qur'an: 28;4.
35. Qur'an: 7;74.
36. Qur'an: 7;80–81.
37. Qur'an: 7;85.
38. Qur'an: 14;4.
39. S. Qutb, *The Mission of Muhammad* (Karachi: Islamic Foundation, n.d.), p. 8.
40. Qur'an: 2;143.
41. S. Qutb, *Milestones*, pp. 10–11.
42. S.A.A. Maududi, *A Short History of the Revivalist Movement in Islam* (Lahore: Islamic Publications, n.d.), pp. 38–39.
43. S. Qutb, *Milestones*, pp. 12–13.
44. S.A.A. Maududi, *The Process of Islamic Revolution* (Lahore: Islamic Publications, n.d.), p. 28.
45. Ibid., p. 26.
46. Qur'an: 2;170.

BIBLIOGRAPHY

Boff, Leonardo. *Jesus Christ Liberator: A Critical Christology of Our Time*. Maryknoll, N.Y.: Orbis Books, 1978.
———. *Church: Charism and Power*. London: SCM, 1985.
Bonino, J.M. *Revolutionary Theology Comes of Age*. London: SPCK, 1975.
Gutiérrez, Gustavo. *A Theology of Liberation*. Maryknoll, N.Y.: Orbis Books, 1974.
Maududi, S.A.A. *The Moral Foundations of the Islamic Movement*. Lahore: Islamic Publications, 1976.
———. *A Short History of the Revivalist Movement in Islam*. Lahore: Islamic Publications, 1976.
———. *Islamic Way of Life*. Kuwait: International Islamic Federation of Student Organizations, 1977.
———. *The Process of Islamic Revolution*. Lahore: Islamic Publications, 1970.
———. *Fundamentals of Islam*. Lahore: Islamic Publications, 1975.
Qutb, S. *The Mission of Muhammad*. Karachi: Islamic Foundation, 1969.
———. *This Religion of Islam*. Kuwait: International Islamic Federation of Student Organizations, 1977.
———. *Islam: The Religion of the Future*. Kuwait: International Islamic Federation of Student Organizations, n.d.
———. *Milestones*. Kuwait: International Islamic Federation of Student Organizations, n.d.

4

Mukti, the Hindu Notion of Liberation

Implications for an Indian Theology of Liberation

SEBASTIAN PAINADATH

In the Second Vatican Council's Declaration on the Relationship of the Church to Non-Christian Religions (*Nostra Aetate*), Hinduism is appraised in the following words:

> In Hinduism men contemplate the divine mystery and express it through an unspent fruitfulness of myths and through searching philosophical inquiry. They seek release from the anguish of our condition through ascetical practices or deep meditation or a loving, trusting flight towards God.[1]

These words of the Council unfold the very core of Hinduism. The basic dynamics of Hinduism consist in (1) a keen awareness of the existential estrangement of the human situation; (2) a relentless quest for release from this estrangement; and (3) an all-pervading sense of the divine as absolute mystery. The quest for liberation emerges out of the awareness of the human predicament and is oriented towards the unfathomable mystery of the Divine. The Hindu understands human life as coming out of the divine source and moving towards the divine goal.[2]

In the process of its evolution, there is an existential estrangement that has to be overcome by the pursuit of meditation, cult, asceticism, and an ethically sound life; but ultimately, liberation is a gift of divine grace. This process of interaction between the divine and the human could take several cycles of life on this earth. The entire human person, with its social, psychological, and spiritual aspects — nay, the entire cosmos — moves towards its final integration into the divine life. Cosmos, humanity and God form a cosmo-theandric unity. The progressive restoration of this unity is the basic dynamic of the Hindu understanding of liberation (*mukti*).

The term *mukti* comes from the Sanskrit root *muc*, which means to deliver, release, set free.[3] *Mukti* is the *state* of being released, set free, liberated, and the *process* of becoming free. The term is used in the Hindu Scriptures to denote both the experience of partial liberation on this earth and the state of ultimate liberation in the Divine life.[4]

LIBERATION ACCORDING TO THE VEDAS

The Vedas (1500–900 B.C.E.) are the inspired source and universal norm of all the sacred Scriptures of Hinduism. The world view of the Vedas is based on the intuitive perception (*manisha*) of reality in its totality and interdependence. God's being is being-in-the-world. It is in creating the world that God came to *be*.[5] The Vedas speak not of a God who creates the world out of nothingness, but of the God who brings forth the world out of God's own *becoming*. A powerful image for this is that of the creative self-immolation of the Creator-God (Prajapati) in the primeval fire.[6] The power that preserves the cosmo-theandric unity is called *rta*.[7] It is the cause of integration in human persons, harmony in society, and order in the universe. Ethical life is, therefore, the human response to the demands of *rta*. Sin is disorder (*anrit*), transgression of the law of reality. Liberation consists in a life of harmony with others, with nature, and ultimately with the divine. The Vedic person had a positive outlook on life and on all joys that life could give: "May the wind blow us joy: may the sun shine down joy on us, may our days pass with joy, may the night be a gift of joyful peace."[8]

"The Vedic optimism is not anthropological but on the whole cosmological ... It starts from a more holistic perspective which views man and cosmos as a dynamic unity in which both are engaged in the very existence of the Universe."[9] Hence, human welfare depends on the cosmic order. For this, however, the human person stands in need of the assistance of the superior beings called *devas*. They are the personified forms of the divine qualities and custodians of the cosmic order. They have to be appeased through rites and rituals, hymns and prayers, dances and feasts. These cultic forms of religious life had thus orginally the purpose of preserving cosmic order and social harmony. But gradually they were manipulated by the dominant priestly class (Brahmins) and converted into magical forms of procuring favours for those who perform them.[10] The transcendent divine thus became idolised in cultic practices, and social life was fragmented into a hierarchial caste structure.

The protest of the spirit against this cultic objectivisation of religion came through the Upanishadic sages.

LIBERATION ACCORDING TO THE UPANISHADS

The Upanishadic masters of spirituality (1000–500 B.C.E.) in their passionate quest for truth, turned into the depth of their own being. "When we pass from the Vedic hymns to the Upanishads we find that the interest shifts from the objective to the subjective, from brooding on the wonder of the outside world to the meditation on the significance of the self. The human self contains the clue to the interpretation of nature. The Real at the heart of the universe is reflected in the infinite depths of the soul."[11]

The Upanishadic Scriptures are the fruits of the contemplative pursuits of the sages of India. According to them, liberation is achieved through intuitive knowledge: "By knowing the Divine we are freed from all fetters!"[12] The fetters are constituted by the deceptive power of *maya* emerging from matter. Human intellect under the impact of *maya* is shrouded by the veil of ignorance (*avidya*). Liberation, therefore, consists in the removal of ignorance and in the consequent awakening of the spirit to the true self in its unity with the Absolute (Brahman).[13]

Hence the Upanishadic Prayer:

> From the unreal lead me to the Real
> From darkness lead me to the Light
> From death lead me to Immortality.[14]

All values related to earthly concerns are subordinated to the supreme value of achieving transcendent wisdom through contemplative pursuits.[15] Upanishads propose basically a way of *Jnana* (gnosis) for attaining liberation. As a result, the Upanishadic schools gradually became rather esoteric in their life and thought. They were cut off from the existential struggles of social life. The contemplative introspection demanded by the spiritual masters was unattainable by ordinary people. The protest of the spirit against the cultic objectivisation of the Vedas and the mystical subjectivisation of the Upanishads came through the great Buddha.

LIBERATION ACCORDING TO BUDDHA

Gautama became the Buddha through the enlightenment experience. This meant for him a deep insight into the mystery of existential suffering and an awareness of liberation (*mukti, moksha*) from it. Reality, according to the Budddhist world view, is a continuous flux, an unceasing becoming. This impermanency (*anicca*) causes suffering (*dukha*), which is the basic character of life. The ontic restlessness gives rise to a passionate desire (*trshna*) that is the immediate cause of suffering in human life. Desire engenders attachment (*upadana*), greed (*kama*), anger (*krodha*), delusion (*moha*), lust (*mada*), aggressivity (*matsarya*), and so forth, and thereby ties down human life to the cyclic process of birth and death (*samsara*). Emancipation from the grips of these causes of suffering and ultimately from the process of rebirth is the Buddhist understanding of liberation.[16]

In order to achieve this liberation, one has to awaken oneself to the true self through meditative praxis. The final state of liberation is *Nirvana*, the definitive "blowing out" of the fire of desire and the "total extinction" of the cause of suffering.[17] Together with the praxis of meditative introspection, Buddha proposes the eightfold way (*marga*) of ethics for liberation: (1) right grasp of reality (*samyag-drshti*); (2) right resolve to follow the truth (*samyag-sankalpa*); (3) right speech in harmony with truth (*samyag-vak*); (4) right action with due respect for life and truth (*samyag-karma*); (5) right livelihood with a morally sound profession (*samyag-ajiva*); (6) right endeavour to conquer evil (*samyag-vyayama*); (7) right mindfulness focussed on the ideal of life (*samyag-smrti*); and (8) right meditation (*samyag-samadhi*).[18]

Buddha does not speak of the Ultimate in theistic categories. This is part of the reason why Buddhism could not strike permanent roots in Hindu India.

This short survey of the understanding of liberation in the classical period of Indian culture has brought out three aspects of the liberative process: (1) The Vedic religion interpreted liberation as emergence from disorder, disharmony and sin; the way to achieve this is *surrender* to the gods through rites and rituals. (2) The Upanishads understood liberation in terms of overcoming the shroud of ignorance and awakening oneself to the true Self in Brahman; the way for this is meditative *introspection* in pursuit of the experience of the Self. (3) For Buddha, liberation consists in transcending the causes of suffering, and the way to that is *meditative praxis* and an *ethically integral life*. These three factors are, in fact, constitutive elements of an integrated spirituality of liberation. A holistic perception of reality through meditative pursuit (*jnana*) is a prerequisite for any spirituality of liberation. Such a perception expresses itself in a total and loving self-surrender (*bhakti*) to the divine, and actualises itself through transformative action (*karma*) in the world. *Jnana, bhakti* and *karma* are the constitutive strands of classical Indian spirituality and the integral elements of an Indian theology of liberation.

An attempt was made by an unknown sage around 400 B.C.E. to bring these three strands together and to evolve a spirituality of liberation. The fruit of his work is the spiritual classic of India, the *Bhagavad Gita*. We shall make a closer study of the notion of liberation in this book.

THE BHAGAVAD GITA

For centuries the *Bhagavad Gita* has existed as part of the great Indian epic *Mahabharata*, but orginally it was an independent mystical poem. The entire text of seven hundred verses is composed in the form of dialogue between Krishna and Arjuna in a chariot on the battlefield of Kurukshetra just before the decisive battle between the Pandavas and the Kauravas. Arjuna, the commander-in-chief of the Pandavas, was overcome by grief and wanted to retreat from the battlefield. Krishna, the charioteer, then opened his vision to a holistic perception of reality and motivated him to "stand up and fight."

This is a highly symbolic scene. Pandavas and Kauravas stand for the forces of justice (*dharma*) and injustice (*adharma*) constantly at war with each other on the battlefield of life.[19]

> The chariot is the classical Indian symbol for the
>   human person:
> The self is the owner of the chariot,
> The chariot is body,
> Intuitive intellect (*buddhi*) is the charioteer,
> Mind (*manah*) the reins that curb it,
> Senses are the steeds.[20]

As the chariot moves on the battlefield, the human person evolves on the battlefield of life, torn between the forces of *dharma* and *adharma*. In moments of crisis, when the human self (*atman*), the owner of the chariot, can no longer master the situation, the divine Lord manifests his presence in the intuitive intellect (*buddhi*) and guides the self on the path of *dharma*. In such moments, all that one can do is totally to "surrender" oneself to the divine Lord (2,7) and follow his words of liberation. Under the impact of the divine "Word and Grace," Arjuna goes through a process of total transformation, which makes him overcome his confusion and depression (18,73). An analysis of this process would clarify the notion of liberation in the *Gita*.

LIBERATION IN THE LIFE OF THE PERSON

According to the *Gita* two ways of life are possible: one determined by egoism (*ahamkara*), or one enlightened by self-awareness (*atmabodha*). Egoism is constituted by desire, craving (*kama*), the possessive attitude of the will. In a life dominated by egoism, one would put oneself at the core of everything and make one's own profit motive the criterion for all (16, 10–16). *Kama* "obscures the right perception of reality" (3,38–39), and is the "fundamental cause of sin" (2,62; 3,41). It is the "ever pursuing enemy of man on this earth" (3,43). Liberation, according to the *Gita*, is ultimately freedom from the grips of *kama*.[21]

The goal of the liberative process is a true awareness of the human self in its union with the divine self (*atmabodha*). "Through meditation see the (human) self in the (divine) Self" (13,25), and "rejoice in the (divine) Self"

(6,20; 3,17). Liberative life is one that is "united with the divine Self" and "freed from *Kama*" (2,48). One who experiences this inner union and freedom would be able to look at oneself and the world from a divine perspective; one sees "all things in the self, and the self in all things" (6,29–31).

In order to achieve this inner liberation the *Gita* proposes a threefold path of spiritual evolution consisting of a holistic vision of reality (*jnana*), a total surrender to the Lord (*bhakti*), and action for the transformation of the world (*karma*). These three factors, as we have seen above, form the integral elements of a spirituality of liberation.[22]

Initially, *jnana, bhakti,* and *karma* would need stimuli from outside: one has to study sacred Scriptures and seek instruction from masters (*Vijnana,* 4,34;16,23–24). Self-surrender to the Lord (*bhakti*) would find expression in offerings (9,26), worship of gods (7,21–22), and rituals (4,24; 9,16,24). The works to be done (*karma*) will have to be assigned by elders or social customs (2,31–33; 16,24). But one has to grow beyond this initial stage of spiritual life, for "not by the study of the Vedas or grim, ascetic practices, not by the giving of alms or sacrifice" can one really reach the Lord (11,53).

As a person grows in a liberative spirituality, there is a progressive interiorization of *jnana, bhakti,* and *karma.* Through the regular practice of meditation (6,10–46), the knowledge communicated by spiritual masters and gained through Scriptures (*vijnana*) is transformed into an experiential perception of the divine (*jnana*). The inner eye of the soul is enlightened (11,8), and the person is enabled to "see oneself in the divine Self, and the Divine in oneself" (13,25; 6,5–6; 3,17). God manifests God's self from the womb of being, from within the "cave of the heart" (13,18; 15,15; 18,61). God reveals God's self as the God who passionately loves the human.

> And now again, give ear to this my highest word,
> of all the most mysterious:
> I love you dearly:
>   hence I tell you all these words
>   for your well being (18,64).

This inner experience of a God who loves us truly liberates the person from the grips of egocentredness (*ahamkara*). Once this experience awakens the core of being, the person is motivated to total self-surrender (*bhakti*) to the Lord of love (*bhagavan*).

Hence the repeated invitation of the Lord in the *Gita*:

> Bear me in your mind, love me and worship me,
> Sacrifice and prostrate yourself to me
> So will you come to me, I promise you truly,
> for you are dear to me.

> Surrender all your concerns to me
>> and take refuge in me alone,
> I shall liberate you from all your sins and evils.
>> Grieve not! (18,65-66).

> In the Lord alone take refuge
>> with all your being.
> By his grace you will attain
>> the highest abode of peace (18,62).

> Let your self be "intent on me" (9,34),
> "let it enter into me" (6,47),
> "be united with me!" (12,11)

External cult evolves into interior self-surrender, for the "temple of the Lord" is experienced within. Life of action (*karma*), too, receives a new freedom from within. As under the impact of *jnana* and *bhakti* — holistic understanding and self-surrender — one is purified, one enjoys a certain liberation from the grips of egoism (*ahamkara*) and from the dominance of the possessive attitudes of the mind (*kama*). One no longer clings to the fruits of action for one's own profit with utmost "commitment and precision" (2,50; cf. also 12,11; 18,6). The work that one has to do in this world is done in an attitude of "surrendering all actions to the Lord" (12,6; 9,27):

> Work is your responsibility:
>> but don't cling to its fruits.

> Be united with the divine and get engaged in action.
> Surrender all attachments,
> be equanimous in success and failure
> Equanimity is truly spirituality. (2,47–48)

As a person reaches integration in spirituality, the three paths of *jnana, bhakti,* and *karma* converge and form a holistic vision and way of life.[23] The divine self that one meditatively experienced within oneself is now seen everywhere (*jnana*), for "the entire cosmos is permeated by the divine presence" (11,38; 9,4; 15,17). "God is the beginning, the middle and the end of the entire creation" (9,18; 10,20). "God is the father of this world, mother, ordainer, Lord, friend, way, home and refuge" (9,17–18) "the life-giving source" (7,10; 14,4; 15,4), "the supporting abode" (9,4; 11,18; 8,22), and the place of final restoration (9,18; 8,21; 7,6). Once the whole world is thus experienced as the "body and temple of the Lord" (13,3; 11,9ff.), one surrenders oneself to the Lord present in the world (*bhakti*): "Knowing me as the source of all, they commune with me in love, fulfilled with warm affection" (10,8).

> He who sees me everywhere
>   and everything in me,
> to him I am not lost,
>   nor is he lost to me.

> He who thus in deep union with me communes in
>   love with me
>   as abiding in all things
> in whatever way of life he be,
>   that integrated man lives-and-moves in me.
>   (6,30-31)

With the world-oriented evolution of *jnana* and *bhakti*, *karma*, too, evolves as a world-affirming dynamism. An integrated person, who perceives the Lord everywhere, is motivated to work with and for the Lord in view of bringing "welfare to all beings" (5,25). This social dimension of the spirituality of the *Gita* needs special attention.

LIBERATION IN THE EVOLUTION OF SOCIETY

The *Gita* was written at a time of sociocultural crisis in Indian society. A dualistic philosophy called *Samkhya* was exerting considerable influence on the people. According to *Samkhya*, reality consisted of two irreconcilable principles of spirit (*purusha*) and matter (*prakriti*). In the human person, the spiritual particle (soul) is entangled in matter; liberation would then mean the emancipation of the spirit from the grips of matter. Any sort of involvement in secular fields of life such as agriculture, trade, political administration, and even family life, would only lead to an increased slavery of the spirit to matter. Hence, the *Samkhya* preacher called upon the people to break their ties with family and society and retire to the solitude of forests for ascetical practices and meditative aloofness.[24] The *Gita* was written to counteract this world-denying spirituality. When read in the living context of the original text, the social relevance of the spirituality of the *Gita* becomes clearer. It is significant that Krishna does not ask Arjuna to leave the turbulent battlefield or to run away from the crisis situation, but to confront it boldly. Arjuna can reach fulfilment only by "standing up and fighting" on the side of *dharma*. The very first phrase of the text makes it clear that the battlefield is really the "battlefield of *dharma*" (1,1).

Dharma is a comprehensive term that gives meaning to personal life and social evolution. This term derives from the Sanskrit root *dhr*, which means to integrate, hold together, support. *Dharma* is, therefore, the state of being held together, harmony and integration. In the life of the individual, *dharma* would mean bodily health, psychic balance, and spiritual realization. In the life of society, *dharma* means justice, love, and harmony. In the total evolution of history, *dharma* is the salvific reality, the meaning-giving centre and eschatological principle. In and through the interaction between the human and the divine, *dharma* evolves in the world and leads everything to final integration. *"Dharma* is that which holds society together; *adharma* is that which breaks society asunder. Anything that makes for the consolidation of society is *dharma*; anything that makes for the disintegration of society is *adharma. Dharma* is that which makes for social coherence."[25]

In the *Gita*, God is the "ultimate foundation" of *dharma* in the world (14,27); the divine power of *dharma* is operative in all beings (7,11). In the evolution of society, God is at work "establishing dharma" (4,8). When humankind, left to itself, cannot push forward the progressive evolution of *dharma* in the face of the oppressive forces of injustice (*adharma*), God intervenes through an incarnational event:

> Unborn am I, changeless in my self
> Of all contingent beings I am the Lord
> Yet by my creative energy I consort with the material
>   nature, which is mine
> and come-to-be in historical time.
> For whenever *dharma* is in the decline
> and *adharma* gets the hand
> then I create myself on this earth.
> For the liberation of the poor
> For the destruction of evil-doers
> for the restoration of *dharma*
> I come into being age after age. (4, 6-8)

This famous text on the incarnational descent of God into the world interprets historical process in terms of the progressive creation of *dharma*. Spirituality consists in human cooperation with the divine work of establishing *dharma*. God is at work in the lives of individuals and in the evolution of society recreating this world; the human person (like Arjuna in the *Gita*) is called upon to cooperate with the Lord in this salvific work (18,66).

The Lord asks Arjuna to get engaged in action for bringing about the "integration of the world" (*lokasamgraha*) (3,20-25) with a "passionate concern for the welfare of all beings" (*sarvabhutahiteratah*) (5,25; 12,4). A person who has gone through the integration process of *jnana, bhakti*, and *karma* would "dedicate the whole being" (18,62) to the divine work of cosmic integration. Such a liberated person is at the disposal of the Lord of history with joy and enthusiasm (6,20; 5,25), involved on working for the liberation of all from the grips of injustice, grief, and misery (3, 20–26; 12,13–20). In a spirit of "self-sacrifice" (*yajna*) that person lives for the welfare of all beings.

The individual who is liberated from enslaving attachments, and whose intellect is enlightened through *jnana*, does everything as an offering to the welfare of the world; that person's life of action reaches integration (4,23).[26]

The *Gita* emphasises that "only action done in terms of self-sacrifice can be liberative" (3,9); "those who cook food for their own sake eat sin!" (3,13).

A PROPHETIC CRITIQUE ON SOCIETY

Creative involvement in the integration of society would demand a critical attitude to all the forces of disintegration. A liberated person knows well that the Lord is at work in the process of "destroying evil-doers" in society (4,8). This awareness creates courage to expose the demonic forces of social structure. The main hindrance in the process of social integration in Indian society has been the rigid caste system. According to the traditional understanding of caste in India, one is born into a particular caste (*jati*), and one's future life and destiny is determined by one's birth. The author of the *Gita* questions this birth-bound interpretation of social stratification. He makes two points clear:[27]

(1) All human beings are ultimately equal, for God is present in them all (9,29 ; 13,18). A liberated person would look at all people from this perspective of human equality: such a person would "view in the self-same way friends and enemies, saints and sinners, the aristocratic Brahmins and the outcastes" (6,9; 5,18; 14,24).

This "equanimous vision" (2,48), which is the essence of the *Gita's* spirituality, breaks down caste barriers and social prejudices. Over against the Brahmanical theory that only people belonging to higher castes could reach God, the *Gita* proclaims that people of the lowest caste (*Sudras*), those born of "sinful wombs," and the "worst of sinners" all can reach the Lord and enter into the ultimate state of realization through the pursuit of an unswerving devotion to the Lord (*bhakti*) (9,30–32; 6,40; 13,26). *Bhakti* breaks through the walls which compartmentalise people into caste structures.

(2) However, differences do exist in the actual social situation of life's evolution. They are not to be evaluated in terms of the family in which a person is born (*jati*), but according to the inherent qualities of life (*gunah*) (18,41–44). A person with high spiritual qualities of a Brahmin may be born of a Sudra womb, and vice versa.[28] The position of a person in society has to be determined by the dominant qualities of the person (4,13). Hence, each one has to assess through critical and meditative introspection the worth of one's personality and discover one's specific *dharma* (*svadharma*) and live accordingly:

> By doing the work that is proper to him, rejoicing in
>   the work, a man succeeds, perfects himself.
> By dedicating the work that is his to do
>   to the Lord who is the real source of all works,

and whose power permeates the entire world,
man attains liberation and perfection.

Better to do one's own work,
   though (apparently) devoid of merit
   than another's however well performed. (18,45-47)

The discovery of one's self-identity (*svabhava*) and the pursuit of one's
specific role in society (*svadharma*) are matters of search and struggle.[29]
The dynamics of this process consist in a dialectical interaction between an
analysis of the forces at work in society (2,42–44; 16,9–20) and a total self-
surrender to the transformative work of the Lord in society (8,7; 9,27).
Liberative action is action "done unto perfection" (2,50) as a creative participation in the work of the Lord: "The man, who sees the work that is
his to do, yet covets not its fruits for himself, is interiorly free, yet creatively
active" (6,1; 18,2).

LIBERATION FROM THE CYCLE OF REBIRTH

A fundamental element of Hinduism is its belief in the spiral process of
rebirth. Whatever be the arguments brought in favour of the theory of
rebirth, it is a fact that the interpretation of the present life in terms of
reparation for the sins of the past life has induced a certain fatalism into
the Hindu outlook on life and crippled to a great extent the courageous
commitment of the people to the change of social structures. The *Gita*
accepts rebirth as a *natural* course of life's evolution (2,13,22,27); but it
points out a *supernatural* way of liberation from this "ocean of birth and
rebirth" (9,3). Even if a person is considered to be "born of sinful wombs"
(9,32) and looked down upon as "the worst of sinners" (4,36), one can be
saved from bondage of the "law of retribution" (*karma*), if in deep interior
union (*jnana*) one surrenders oneself to the Lord (*bhakti*) and works for
the promotion of *dharma* (*karma*).[30]

Those who cast off all their works on me, solely intent on me, and
meditate on me in spiritual exercise, leaving no room for other, and
so really do me honour, these will I lift up on high out of the ocean
of recurring death, and that right soon, for their thoughts are fixed
on me. (12,6–7)

Ultimately, liberation is a work of divine grace. The human person can
only dispose the self to receive the divine light and grace (2,7; 11,4). It is
the divine Lord who confers on the human the light of wisdom (*jnana*,
11,10, 11,7), moves the heart with the divine power of love (*bhakti*, 12,13–
20; 18,64–65; 9,31), and motivates the devotee to liberative action (*karma*,

8,7; 18,56): "with my grace you shall overcome all hindrances and reach the ultimate abode of peace" (18,56,58,62).

What is the ultimate state of salvation? The *Gita* does not speak of it monistically in terms of the annihilation of the individual human self in the divine. The liberated human self "goes to the Lord" (7,23; 8,15: 11,55), "attains Him" (8,7; 18,65), and "lives in the Lord" (12,8) without "losing its identity" (6,30,40; 9,31). The human person reaches ultimate fulfilment in the communion of love with the divine Lord:

> In all contingent being I am equally present;
>   I hate none, nor is anyone specially dear to me.
> But those who commune with me in love, they are in me,
>   and I am in them. (9,29)

MUKTI, ITS IMPLICATIONS FOR A THEOLOGY OF LIBERATION

The following aspects of the Hindu understanding of liberation (*mukti*) are of significance for developing an integrated theology of liberation:

(1) *A holistic vision of reality.* Right from the beginning, Hinduism showed a keen sense for the totality of reality. Humanity, the material universe, and the divine form a cosmo-theandric unity. The Vedic perception of the cosmic principle (*rta*), the Upanishadic insight into the Absolute (*Brahman*) and the *Gita's* understanding of total integration (*dharma*) point to this unity of reality. One has to experience this unity "by seeing all things in one's own self, and one's own self in all things."[31] Integral liberation is possible only in terms of restoring this unity. Hence *theological, anthropological* and *ecological* aspects of life must find articulation in a theology of liberation. Human progress at the cost of destroying nature is no progress at all. If the embryo eats up the uterus, its life itself is threatened. The *Gita's* perception of the cosmos as the "body of the Lord" (11,9ff.; 13,3; 7,7–12) and its insistence on love and concern for *all beings* (12,13; 5,25; 12,4) call forth a cosmological perspective in a theology of liberation. And the human person cannot attain ultimate liberation without becoming oriented to the divine. Mere emancipation from economic and political bondage is not total human liberation.

(2) *The call to personal integration.* Hinduism has a deep concern for the integral growth of the individual person. The ascetical prescriptions, ethical norms, and meditation methods proposed by the spiritual masters of India are primarily meant to help the individual reach personal liberation and integration. In the Indian spiritual heritage, there is the deep insight that only a liberated person can liberate others.[32] The *Gita's* way of *jnana, bhakti,* and *karma* offers in this regard an excellent synthesis of spirituality. These three are, in fact, constitutive factors of a spirituality of liberation. Commitment to society (*karma*) can be liberative only if the person is freed

from egoism and enabled to "see the Lord in all things" (*jnana*), and moved to "surrender the self totally to the Lord in love" (*bhakti*). Involvement in social liberation without genuine work at personal liberation would only lead to altered structures of oppression.

A theology of liberation has to be constantly revitalised by a spirituality of liberation.

(3) *The challenge of social liberation.* Hinduism has been often criticised for its overemphasis on the individual's salvation. Under the pressure of casteism and the dualistic doctrine of some of the spiritual leaders of Hinduism, the social dimension of religious experience was, to a great extent, underplayed. But, as the Hindu reformers of the last two centuries have testified through their writings and their radical commitment to social change, there is an undercurrent of social concern in the Hindu scriptures and spiritual traditions.[33] The notion of liberation (*mukti*) is not totally negative toward the values of earthly well-being and social change. Hindu ethics universally demand that the human person reaches final salvation (*moksha*) only through the right (*dharma*) use of material goods (*artha*) and proper channelling of psychic energies (*kama*).[34] The *Gita's* understanding of *dharma* is of unique significance in developing a theology of liberation. The personal, social, and eschatological aspects of the dynamic of liberation form a unity in *dharma*. The integration of the individual is possible only through participation in the creation of *dharma* in society. It would be theologically significant to reflect on this term in connection with the demands of the Kingdom of God proclaimed by Jesus.[35]

(4) *Liberation as an interreligious project.* Hinduism has basically a soteriological structure, at the centre of which emerges the experience of a God becoming human (*avatara*). All rites and rituals, hymns and prayers, feasts and festivals somehow express the quest for liberation and communicate the experience of God saving humankind. In recent years, Hindu leaders have been paying special attention to revitalising the social dimension of this process of liberation. At heart, Hinduism is open to other religions and is willing to assimilate the positive values of other religions. The promotion of liberation, both in praxis and in theological reflection, must be an interreligious concern. We are living in a new age of the spirit, an age in which religions and cultures are constantly being challenged to put human concern at the centre and to work together for the integral well-being and total liberation of humankind. "In the world today, there is a need for all religions to collaborate in the cause of humanity, and to do this from the viewpoint of the spiritual nature of man ... And what India offers specifically is a noble spiritual vision of man, man a pilgrim of the Absolute, travelling towards a goal, seeking the face of God."[36]

NOTES

1. *Nostra Aetate*, 2.
2. "That from which all things are born, that by which when born they live,

that into which when dying they enter, That you should desire to know: that is *Brahman*" (*Taittiriya Upanishad*, 3.1).

3. See Monier-Williams, *A Sanskrit-English Dictionary* (Delhi, 1984), s.v. *muc.*

4. M. Dhavamony, *Classical Hinduism* (Rome: Gregorian University Press, 1982), p. 417.

5. *Rig Veda*, 10.129.1.

6. *Satapadabrahmana*, 13.7.1.1.

7. *Rig Veda*, 1.24.8; 10.133.6; 7, 86.

8. *Atharva Veda*, 7.69. "For a hundred autumns may we see, for a hundred autumns may we live, for a hundred autumns may we know, for a hundred autumns may we rise, for a hundred autumns may we flourish, for a hundred autumns may we become, and ever more than a hundred autumns" (*Atharva Veda*, 19.67).

9. Raimundo Panikkar, *The Vedic Experience* (London: Darton, Longman and Todd, 1977), p. 238.

10. *Satapadabrahmana*, 9, 5, 1, 12; 2.2.8–14; 8, 6, 1, 10; 9, 4, 4, 15.

11. S. Radhakrishnana, *The Principal Upanishads* (London, 1924), p. 50.

12. *Svetasvatara Upanishad*, 1.8; 1.11; *Brihadaranyaka Upanishad*, 2.4.5.

13. *Brihadaranyaka Upanishad*, 3.7.23.

14. Ibid., 1.3.28.

15. P. Deussen, *Philosophy of the Upanishad* (London, 1908), p. 364–66. R. Tiwari, *Secular, Social and Ethical Values of the Upanishad* (Delhi, 1985), p. 425.

16. T. Kochumuttom, "Buddhist Notion and Process of Human Liberation," in Paul Puthanangady, ed., *Towards an Indian Theology of Liberation* (Bangalore, 1986), pp. 137–57.

17. See Buddhist Scriptures, *Suttanipata*, 235; *Udana*, 33; *Digha Nijaya*, 2, 266

18. Taitetsu Unno, "Eightfold Path," in Mircea Eade, ed., *The Encyclopedia of Religion*, vol. 5 (New York: Macmillan and Free Press, 1987), pp. 69–71.

19. "Mahabharata is not history, it is a *dharma-grantha*, work treating religious and ethical questions . . . The battlefield here is primarily the one inside the human body . . . The physical battle is only an occasion for describing the battlefield of the human body" (Mahatma Gandhi, *The Bhagavad Gita* [Delhi: Orient Books, 1983], pp. 15–16). "The Bhagavad Gita gives utterance to the aspirations of the pilgrims of all sects who seek to tread the inner way to the city of God. We touch reality most deeply, where men struggle, fail, and triumph" (S. Radhakrishnan, *The Bhagavad Gita* [Delhi, 1977], p. 11).

20. *Katha Upanishad*, 3.3.4.

21. S. Painadath, "Die Bhagavad-Gita, Ein indischer Weg zu Gott und zur Gotteserfahrung," *Geist und Leben* 4 (1982): 288–93.

22. The Sanskrit word *bhakti* comes from the root *bhaj*, which means to share, to participate. *Bhakti* is therefore the attitude of sharing one's life with the Lord in response to the Lord sharing his life with man (4, 3).

23. Aurobindo, *Essays on the Gita* (Pondicherry, 1980), pp. 308–322.

24. G.S. Khair, *Quest for the Original Gita* (Bombay, 1969), pp. 143–44.

25. S. Radhakrishnan, *Occasional Speeches, 1952-56*, p. 23, quoted in A.B. Creel, *Dharma in Hindu Ethics* (Calcutta, 1977), p. 85.

26. "All actions performed for the good or service of others are forms of *yajna* (Mahatma Gandhi, *The Bhagavad Gita*, p. 75).

27. Francis D'Sa, "Caste, Symbol or System?" *Negations* 1 (1982): 116–21. H. S. Sinha, *Communism and Gita* (Delhi, 1979), pp. 154–77.

28. "If the qualities of truth, forgiveness, good conduct, gentleness, austerity, mercy, etc. are seen in a person born of a Sudra family, he is not a Sudra, but a Brahmin." *Mahabharata*, 8, 177, 16, 20–21. Cf. *Manusmriti* 11, 65.

29. S. Painadath, "The Idea of a Salvific Community in the Bhagavad Gita," *Jeevadhara* 12 (1982): p. 309.

30. Cf. *Gita*, 4.36–41; 13.13; 13.29; 8.16; 8.13; 18.56; 2.50–51.

31. *Isa Upanishad*, 6; *Gita*, 6, 29.

32. Aurobindo, *Essays on the Gita*, pp. 543–552.

33. Antony Chirappanath, "Indian Renaissance and Liberation," in Paul Puthanangady, ed., *Towards an Indian Theology of Liberation*, pp. 158–77.

34. S. Radhakrishnan, *Eastern Religions and Western Thought* (London: Allen & Unwin, 1954), chapters 9 and 3.

35. See George Soares Prabhu, "The Dharma of Jesus," Bible-*bhashyam* 6 (1980): 358–81; Francis D'Sa, "Dharma as Delight in Cosmic Welfare, A Study of Dharma in the Gita," ibid.: pp. 335–57: K. Luke, "Righteousness/Dharma," ibid.: pp. 311–34.

36. John Paul II, speech to the representatives of religious, cultural, social, economic and political life of India at Delhi on 2 February 1986, in *Pope Speaks to India* (Bombay, 1986), pp. 46, 48.

5

Engaged Buddhism

Liberation from a Buddhist Perspective

SULAK SIVARAKSA

At present, there is no such thing as a solid global-scale Buddhist liberative vision. Unlike disciples of other great world religions, Buddhists have no recognized international religious leaders like the Pope to prescribe specific dogmas on social justice for the faithful. Nor do Buddhists have an international organization like the World Council of Churches or the World Muslim League whose resolutions often have an impact on various local communities. Although the present Dalai Lama is greatly revered, he is the spiritual head of the Tibetan tradition only. As a result, perhaps, Buddhists have not been at the forefront in planning desirable societies, nor, it should be added, can any Buddhist community be considered as an ideal example.

It appears, too, that, as is the case with all religions, there are some Buddhists who can claim spiritual happiness despite the fact that in many so-called Buddhist countries, the majority of people face enormous suffering.

Thus, it may be easy for those who have not made a profound study of Buddhism to fall into the belief that Buddhism is merely a way of personal salvation for escapists in search of spiritual enlightenment.

This, however, is an erroneous assumption. Buddhism strongly asserts that social imperfections can be reduced by the reduction of greed, hatred, and ignorance, and by compassionate action guided by wisdom. In the *Anguttara Nikaya* (Gradual Sayings), the Buddha is quoted as saying:

> He who has understanding and great wisdom does not think of harming himself or another, nor of harming both alike. He rather thinks of his own welfare, and that of others, and that of both, and of the

welfare of the whole world. In that way one shows understanding and great wisdom.

Examination of the Buddha's messages on compassion show that he was certainly not indifferent to human suffering. Buddhists are taught to believe that social misery can be remedied, at least partly. The Buddha's discourses in the *Digha Nikaya* demonstrate that early Buddhists were very much concerned with the creation of social conditions favorable to the cultivation of Buddhist values.

Buddhist teachings, such as the insistence on the interrelatedness of all life, and the ideals of compassion for all beings and nonviolence, have been leading some contemporary Buddhists to broader and deeper interpretations of the relationship between social, environmental, racial, and sexual justice and peace, and have inspired them to become engaged in today's society by attempting to come to grips with, and work towards solving, some of the problems which exist.

Ken Jones, a well-known Buddhist activist from the United Kingdom, writes the following:

> The task of Buddhists in both East and West in the 21st century is to interpret Buddhism in terms of the needs of industrial-age man and woman in the social conditions of their time, and to demonstrate its acute and urgent relevance to the ills of that society.[1]

In this respect, people need to know how to apply the four Noble Truths and the Noble Eightfold Path today in the context of their surroundings, and how these methods can inspire people to work towards the creation of a desirable society in the future.

Liberation theology and engaged Buddhism have many more similarities than differences, and it is my hope that increased understanding through greater communication and mutual respect will open the door further to a constructive coordination of efforts against the forces of oppression in an interreligious context.

INDIVIDUAL VERSUS SOCIAL KARMA

In the opening chapter of this book, Deane Ferm expresses the view of liberation theologians that sin and evil are both personal and systemic. Engaged Buddhists are also of this opinion, and much has been written on this topic.

The Dalai Lama states,

> Everybody talks about peace, justice, equality, but in practice it is very difficult. This is not because the individual person is bad but because

the overall environment, the pressures, the circumstances are so strong, so influential.

The common notion of "progress" is incomplete. This is reflected in the fact that "development" in the Third World is generally thought of in terms of economic development only, which results in the frequently observed phenomenon of the rich getting richer while the poor become even poorer. This is true for nations and individuals. And of course, no one is happy. Many of the present social systems lead to human rights abuses, a widening gap between the rich and the poor, environmental degradation, and the aggressive destruction of natural resources.

Much of the world's suffering, then, is instigated and perpetuated by social systems and values, and it follows that not only individual growth, but fundamental changes in these systems must be encouraged and pursued.

Buddhadasa Bhikkhu, a well-known and respected Buddhist scholar, writes, "Because the context of these [global] problems is social and not just individual, we must turn our attention to the source of the problem: society."[2]

On this subject, Ken Jones states:

Specific to time and place, different social cultures arise, whether of a group, a community, a social class or a civilization. The young are socialized to their inherited culture. Consciously and unconsciously, they assimilate the norms of approved behavior — what is good, what is bad and what is "the good life" for that culture.

The social karma — the establishment of conditioned behavior patterns — of a particular culture is not simply the aggregate of the karma of the individuals who comprise that culture. . . .

Buddhist social action is justified ultimately . . . by the existence of social as well as individual karma. Immediately, it is simply concerned with relieving suffering; ultimately in creating social conditions which will favor the ending of suffering through the individual achievement of transcendent wisdom.[3]

Bearing in mind that the cycles of oppression in this world must be broken socially as well as personally, the following section contains an analysis of some of the current problems facing the world today as well as of the social systems and values that cause or sustain them.

CURRENT GLOBAL PROBLEMS

Obviously, it is impossible in this one chapter to analyze all of the problems existing in the world today. To simplify the examination of the present human predicament, it might be helpful to look at problems and the social institutions and values that perpetuate them, in the context of the Buddhist concept of the three root causes of suffering — greed, delusion, and hatred.

GREED

Consumer culture and technology are being used to replace spiritual virtues with new values. Greed is now encouraged. Ill-begotten wealth and power are to be admired. So-called "development models" often serve to propagate the message of "the richer the better, the bigger the better, the quicker the better." They degrade human beings and leave no room for spiritual development or respect for indigenous local cultures. Advertising, for the consumer culture, is the new gospel for "progress" in economic development.

This modernization has forced peasants to depend on the market for clothing, electricity, water, fuel, construction materials, fertilizers, pesticides, livestock, and agricultural tools, rather than allowing them to live in the self-sufficient cooperative manner in which they once did.

Greed has brought about the large-scale depletion of natural resources, the majority of which have gone to benefit the "advanced" societies in Japan and the West and the privileged elite in third-world areas, and not for consumption by the peasantry. The poor are gradually losing their land through debt, and millions flock to urban centers each year. In Thailand, young women work as servants or unskilled factory workers, or are forced into prostitution. Indeed, the country has more prostitutes than monks. As people pour into the cities, industry cannot absorb them, and many are forced to resort to crime.

Zen writer David Brandon has this to say of the present situation:

> Cravings have become cemented into all forms of social structures and institutions. People who are relatively successful at accumulating goods and social position wish to ensure that they remain successful. Both in intended and unintended ways they erect barriers of education, finance and law to protect their property and other interests. These structures and their protective institutions continue to exacerbate and amplify the basic human inequalities in housing, health care, education and income. They reward greed, selfishness and exploitation rather than love, sharing and compassion. Certain people's lifestyles, characterized by greed and overconsumption, become dependent on the deprivation of the many. The oppressors and the oppressed fall into the same trap.[4]

Buddhadasa Bhikkhu, who preaches and writes for the liberation of all human beings, has vehemently criticized materialism, especially the worship of money and technology. While denouncing blind technological progress, the consumer culture, militarism, and multinational corporations, he has also condemned mainstream education and mass media for promoting greed. Proper education, he feels, should go beyond the intellect to link the heart and the mind to reduce self-centeredness and encourage self-lessness. He urges us to live in such a way that we consume appropriately rather than excessively, and to return to the true essence of our spiritual teachings.

Many Christian groups have done studies on multinational corporations and international banking. Buddhists should learn from them and use these findings to form a Buddhist position.

It should be noted here that greed for money or power is not ingrained solely in the capitalist system. It pervades all walks of life, and its effects can be seen today in suffering throughout the world.

DELUSION

In order to lead a meaningful life, one must be conditioned by righteous-ness (*dhamma*). If we are not mindful, our lives become conditioned by fear or the search for fame or hedonism, neither of which can be satisfied. This is a path of pure heedlessness, rooted in ignorance and delusion, and many in our society have fallen victim to it. For example, the majority of politicians work only for their own political ends. Some even misuse certain passages of the Scriptures to support their position. In many parts of the world, polit-ical power is used to oppress various social groups such as women, political opponents, racial and religious communities, and the poor.

When the essence of spiritual teachings is misunderstood or deliberately misinterpreted, considerable harm can be done in the name of religion. Buddhism, often linked with politics, has been used to maintain the status quo. Those who are suffering are told to be complacent about their situa-tion, as it is the inevitable result of bad karma in previous lives. The Bud-dhist monkhood has even been used to legitimize the military who act as the main forces of oppression in some areas.

Thus, engaged Buddhists feel that religion must offer spiritual guidance applicable to today's crises. Religion's meaning must not be lost in ritual or politics if we are to achieve true progress as a species.

HATRED

Buddhism teaches us that even if we are struggling against oppression, we must not hate the oppressor. Evil can never be countered constructively with evil. The *Dhammapada* says, "Never by hatred is hatred appeased, but it is appeased by kindness." "One should conquer anger through kindness, wickedness through goodness, selfishness through charity and falsehood through truthfulness." This does not imply that one must lie down and accept oppression. It merely points out that violence is not a viable answer, even as a last resort.

Hatred in its most violent form leads to war. This hatred is often fanned by those in power who have their own masked stakes in a war. Costs of violent conflicts in terms of money, manpower, and lives have been outrageous, all in the name of defending ourselves from each other. Human rights are often forgotten when we are consumed with hatred. We are no longer able to see the interrelatedness of all life that Buddhism preaches.

It seems, then, that the three root causes of suffering — greed, delusion, and hatred — and the social institutions and norms that support them must be dealt with alongside their effects or symptoms, such as poverty, human rights violations, and discrimination.

In order for Buddhists effectively to tackle the problems existing in the world today, we must first determine where we want to go. Each religious tradition must understand its own ideals before its adherents can effectively put them into practice. The next section, therefore, is concerned with the ideal society from a Buddhist perspective.

THE IDEAL SOCIETY

It may be helpful to use the traditional *sila,* or basic rules for Buddhist morality, as a framework for building desirable societies. They are:

(1) to abstain from killing;

(2) to abstain from stealing;

(3) to abstain from sexual misconduct;

(4) to abstain from false speech;

(5) to abstain from intoxicants that cause heedlessness.

These are not commandments. Rather, they are guiding principles that can be voluntarily undertaken to help one lead a more socially just life. To practice them is to be endowed with five ennobling virtues, namely:

(1) loving kindness and compassion;

(2) right means of livelihood and generosity;

(3) sexual restraint;

(4) truthfulness and sincerity;

(5) mindfulness and heedfulness.

Living in such a way would allow one to achieve true human development.

There is no doubt that peace, happiness, and freedom are the supreme goals of Buddhism. All three are synonyms for Nibbana or Nirvana. Thai Buddhist scholar and writer Phra Devavedi (Prayudh Payutto) has much to say regarding liberation and has set out four levels of freedom that lead to the realization of Nibbana.[5] Progression from one level to the next depends on the attainment of the preceding level. The four levels are:

(1) Physical freedom. The basic needs of life must be met (i.e. food, shelter, clothing and health care). And one must be safe from life-threatening calamities and unfavorable natural conditions which implies a positive environment and the wise use of natural resources, life and technology so

as to enhance the quality of life for all while not allowing man to become a slave to these quests.

(2) Social freedom. This category includes freedom from oppression, persecution, exploitation, injustice, discrimination, violence and conflict. This means that one must have good relationships with others as well as full human rights, equality, tolerance and a cooperative outlook.

(3) Emotional freedom. This level refers to a state of freedom from all mental defilements and suffering which leaves one purified, secure and profoundly happy and peaceful. For example, to attain this level of freedom, one would have to be endowed with love, compassion, confidence, mindfulness, conscience, generosity, forbearance and tranquility.

(4) Intellectual freedom. This is freedom through knowledge and wisdom without any distortion, bias or ulterior motives; the cultivation of the insight into the true nature of things.

The third and fourth levels can be combined under the heading "spiritual freedom." Ideally, all people should have the right to conditions which might allow them to realize Nibbana. Many liberation theologians have expressed similar views. Buddhists can support the kind of grassroots theology in the Christian liberation tradition and take inspiration from it—particularly the flow of cooperation, communication, and inspiration between the "popular, pastoral and professional" levels. However, Buddhists have not adopted a "preferential option for the poor" and are encouraged to work towards the reduction of suffering for all those who are oppressed.

It has been said that ideal conditions can be realized through righteous ruling. In any society, leaders or coordinators must emerge. Buddhism regards politics as a necessary evil in which the rulers and the ruled must not exploit each other or their environment. Political institutions should act as a framework where justice, peace, mercy, equality, decency, friendliness, and basic human rights can prevail. Politics, on the one hand, gives powers and legitimation to the rulers to use a set of laws to run the country in the name of, and for the benefit of, the people who are being ruled. On the other hand, if people refuse that authority or question that legitimacy, the rulers no longer have the right to rule. This last statement is a basic Buddhist concept regarding national politics. It was quoted by Mongkut, the first "modern" Siamese king to open his country to the West in the 1850s. Many believe that this open-door policy allowed us to remain independent while our neighbors were colonized by the great Western powers.

In Buddhism, there are ten *dhamma* of kingship. They are:

dana (generosity)	*tapo* (self-restraint)
sila (morality)	*akkodha* (non-anger)
pariccaga (liberality)	*avihimsa* (non-hurtfulness)
ajjava (uprightness)	*khanti* (forbearance)
maddava (gentleness)	*avirodhana* (non-opposition)

This is the ideal, and not what has happened historically in Buddhist lands. There has been only one leader who ruled righteously in the true Buddhist sense—Emperor Ashoka of India. Buddhist scholar Walpola Rahula has this to say about Ashoka's reign (274–236 B.C.E.):

Buddhism arose in India as a spiritual force against social injustices, against degrading superstitious rites, ceremonies and sacrifices; it denounced the tyranny of the caste system and advocated the equality of all men; it emancipated women and gave her complete spiritual wisdom.[6]

Political power, then, should be used to fashion and sustain a society whose citizens are free to live in dignity, harmony, and mutual respect, free from the degradation of poverty and war.

Right leadership will also include right economic policy. E. F. Schumacher, in his book *Small is Beautiful,* explains the essence of Buddhist economics as follows:

While the materialist is mainly interested in goods, the Buddhist is mainly interested in liberation. . . . The keynote of Buddhist economics is simplicity and non-violence. . . . It is a question of finding the right path of development, the Middle Way, between materialist heedlessness and traditional immobility, in short, of finding "Right Livelihood."[7]

Buddhist economics, according to Schumacher, would involve a sufficient range of material goods (and no more), production based on appropriate technology, and harmony with the environment.

Prominent Thai economist Puey Ungphakorn, one of the first in Thailand to praise E. F. Schumacher's book, set forth a program for the correct development path of a nation. To start with, an efficient society, liberty for the people, and justice are required, and the people must care for one another. Then what he terms four "virtues" necessary for right development are peace within and without (which implies good administration), worthy development goals, well-planned developmental procedures, and power both carefully used and properly checked. Finally, he sees the goals of development to be increased income and improved health standards, economic stability, and equitable distribution of the fruits of production.

In an ideal Buddhist society, under righteous and effective administration, there would be no poverty. Everyone would enjoy economic self-reliance and self-sufficiency, except for the community of monks and nuns who would be deliberately sustained by the lay society's surplus of material resources, in order that lay people could be guided by the clergy's lifestyles and spiritual progress over life and death. In addition to a religious tradition of social ethics, a spirit of nonalignment, a respect for local culture and customs, and a commitment to decentralization would contribute to an Asian model of a just society—with less affluence, perhaps, but with more self-respect and freedom.

Buddhist social action must be directed towards realizing Buddhist ideals. These Buddhist ideals have much in common with the ideals of other religious communities. Meaningful communication and cooperation leading to an interreligious solidarity in striving towards common values would certainly be beneficial to all involved. Thus, exchange and learning between Buddhists and non-Buddhists should be encouraged.

One of the main driving forces behind engaged Buddhism is compassion. The question is how to use compassion and other Buddhist principles to deal with global problems and work towards a more ideal society where all citizens have the right to realize Nibbana. The next section examines possible paths leading from the present conditions in society towards the realization of a better future.

THE PATH—A SOCIALLY ENGAGED SPIRITUALITY

OBJECTIVES

The secular humanist activist and the engaged Buddhist contemplate social action in a fundamentally different way. Buddhadasa Bhikkhu explains it in the following way:

> From the worldly standpoint, development can proceed when desires are increased or satisfied. From the religious standpoint, the more desires can be reduced, the further development can proceed.[8]

Thus, Buddhism seeks to liberate us from our own grasping desires as well as from external oppression.

In the past, development has ignored faith and culture—both vital sources of human values. Activists, even those of agnostic tendency, should try to remain open to the liberative dimensions of these institutions. Even the self-help ideology of grassroots development needs to be reoriented to the local context. Peasants, fishermen, industrial workers, women, and all oppressed factions in any country should be encouraged to explore their religion and the roots of their culture in order to draw inspiration and sustenance from them.

At the same time, we should strengthen and extend the liberation potential within the Buddhist tradition to make it relevant to today's world, and to allow each local community to gain a global perspective, making each aware of global problems, especially the suffering of the poor. If more people were conscious of the problem, it could be solved more efficiently. Further, people suffering under similar oppression should be encouraged to come together to share their experience and insights and to coordinate actions.

We need a better understanding of society and its systems on all levels. For example, much of the trend towards consumerism is fostered or controlled by multinational corporations. If people cannot understand the cause of suffering, they cannot put an end to it.

In this day and age, we do not need to expend more energy gaining converts for our religions. What we need, beyond a return to our own spiritual and cultural core, is conscientization and solidarity, to join with friends of various religious and cultural backgrounds, to work towards social justice. In this aspect, we can learn from liberation theology with its theory of grassroots conscientization, organization, and coordination. However, we need to enlighten not only the oppressed, but also those who are working in multinational corporations, exploitative industries, international banking, unjust governments, and bureaucracies, so that they come to understand that unjust economic systems and indiscriminate use of high technologies are as harmful to those who propagate them as to those subjected to them. Poisonous food, dangerous medicines, or chemical production and the arms race may bring their creators wealth, but eventually they will also become victims. In addition, concerned first-worlders must link themselves meaningfully with those of the Third World to create a more effective movement towards global awareness.

While trying to educate the rich and powerful, we must always communicate with the poor and oppressed. Indeed, if we must choose sides, we should be with the poor, share their suffering, remain humble, and learn from them, especially regarding their culture and lifestyle. The simpler our livelihood is, the less our natural resources will be exploited. The less we imitate the rich, the more we will be free from the harmful effects of consumer culture and high technology. If, through conscientization, we could learn along with the poor not to join the rich people's club or any system of oppression, then it would be the first step away from *economic* development towards full *human* development. This would not really involve a new lifestyle, but a return to our spiritual traditions.

Once our awareness is raised, we must not be afraid to speak out against oppression or war, and participate in the solution.

As Buddhists, we should promote the study and discussion of major social issues (for example, those pertaining to war, the environment, human rights, economics and right livelihood, technology, discrimination, medicine, mass media, education, crime, and intoxicants) in order to formulate appropriate Buddhist responses, and then act together with friends who are seeking similar changes from inside and outside our heritage.

The Role of the Sangha

Unlike the lay community, the Sangha reverses the process of degeneration of the human race described in the Buddhist creation myths: coercion is replaced by cooperation, private property by propertylessness, family and home by the community of wanderers of both sexes, hierarchy by egalitarian democracy. The Sangha symbolizes the unification of means and ends in Buddhist philosophy. That is, the movement working for the resolution of conflict must embody a sane and peaceful process itself. The discipline of the early monastic Sangha was designed to channel expected conflicts of interest among the monks and nuns into processes of peaceful democratic resolution. In order to spread peace and stability in their societies, the monastic Sangha sought to establish moral hegemony over the state, to guide their societies with a code of nonviolent ethics in the interest of social welfare.

However, since the passing away of the Buddha some 2,530 years ago, the historical Sangha has been divided vertically and horizontally by cultural, economic, and political alliances. Sectors of the Sangha in many different countries became dependent on state patronage for their growing communities. With the growth of monastic wealth and land-holding came the integration of the Sangha into society as a priest-class of teachers, ritual performers, and chanters of magic formulas—a sector of the landowning elite with its own selfish interests and tremendous cultural power.

With centralization and hierarchization of the Sangha came increasing elite and state control, so that instead of applying the ethics of nonviolence to the state, a part of the Sangha was increasingly called upon to rationalize violence and injustice.

On the other hand, at the base of society, frequently impoverished and poorly educated, there have always been propertyless and familyless radical clergy who maintain the critical perspective of the Buddha. To this day, scattered communities of Buddhists continue in a radical disregard, and sometimes fiery condemnation, of the official "State Buddhism" with its elite hierarchical structures and its legacies of secular accommodation and corruption.

In looking to the future of humankind, it is, therefore, necessary to look back and place the state and its elites, with their natural tendency towards acquisitive conflict, under the hegemony of the popular institutions that embody the process of nonviolent, democratic, conflict resolution. In traditional Buddhist terms, the king should always be under the influence of the Sangha, and not vice versa.

It is imperative that we support the radical clergy in maintaining this critical perspective of the Buddha. We should wholeheartedly support the Sangha in its efforts to lead the local communities towards self-reliance and away from domination by the elites or their consumerism, and stand together with them to denounce unjust systems.

Indeed, many of the local and agrarian societies still have nonviolent means of livelihood, and respect for each individual as well as for animals, trees, rivers, and mountains.

Although the government and multinational corporations have introduced various technological "advances" and chemical fertilizers and have advertised to make villagers turn away from their traditional ways of life and opt for jeans, Coca Cola and fast food as well as worship of the state and its warlike apparatus, their efforts have been successfully countered by those of the critical Sangha. Some of them have even reintroduced meditation practices for farmers and established rice banks and buffalo banks which are owned by the communities and are for their benefit. Monks are also currently involved in traditional medicine projects among the people, and have even gained recognition from the Public Health Ministry in Thailand. This movement promises to evolve into an alternative road to development — a grassroots Buddhist development model.

HOPEFUL SIGNS

Along with the efforts of some members of the Sangha in Thailand to become involved in social and development work, there are many other positive signs in Buddhism today. Although it would be impossible to mention all of them, here are a few examples:

The Vietnamese monk, Thich Nhat Hanh, is a very well-known engaged Buddhist. His Order of Interbeing is designed to explicitly address social justice and peace issues, sensitizing people to test their behavior in relation to the needs of the larger community, while freeing them from limiting patterns. In directing the individual to focus on his or her interconnection with other beings, Thich Nhat Hanh is asking us to experience the continuity between the inner and outer world, and to act in collaboration and in mutuality with others in the dynamic unfolding of the truth that nurtures justice and creates peace.

Buddhadasa Bhikkhu and his Garden of Liberation in southern Thailand has urged a return to authentic Buddha-dhamma, replacing merit-making with a serious quest for Nibbana, the memorization of Abhidhamma philosophy with an understanding of the Suttas, the performance of magical rituals with the practice of meditation, and an emphasis on the monk with concern for the entire community, lay and monastic.

The Buddhist Peace Fellowships in many Western countries seem to have put Buddhist practice into proper perspective by attempting to improve individually members as well as society and their surroundings, collectively. Rather than sitting on the fence, they have taken a firm Buddhist stand for justice through loving kindness and nonviolence.

Positive action has also been taken by some Japanese Buddhist monks in their movement against armaments and nuclear war. They have worked in Sri Lanka towards reconciliation and have become involved in a number of human rights issues within their country and internationally. Also, the Rishokosakai organization in Japan has established the Niwano Press Prize and the Niwano Foundation to encourage studies toward a peaceful world.

Many promising projects have recently been initiated in the field of alternative education. An example here in Thailand is Dr. Prawase Wasi's village school in Kanchanaburi, about 125 miles west of Bangkok. The school is recognized by the Thai government. Yet, it stresses love and freedom rather than academic competition and applies Buddhist principles of critical self-awareness. Rather than focusing exclusively on the scholarly attainment of higher education, this school promotes self-reliance, good neighborliness, righteous livelihood, contentment, the ability to adapt to the natural environment, and the appreciation of folk arts and indigenous culture.

The Sarvodaya Shramadana Movement in Sri Lanka tries to apply Buddhist principles to awaken people first individually and then at village and national levels. It encourages self-reliance, using appropriate technology and cooperation. However, the movement has been criticized as having a more rhetorical rather than practical approach and has been accused of doing nothing to solve the Sinhalese-Tamil conflicts in the country.

Hong Kong may not appear to be very Buddhistic, but many Buddhist nuns in that country have achieved the highest levels of scholarship. In Sri Lanka, too, research has been conducted by leading Buddhist women regarding their own role. This reminds us that we should explore further the position of women in religion without becoming defensive or clinging to outdated misconceptions. Inequality between the sexes needs to be examined within each spiritual tradition as well as in society in general.

One of the inefficiencies of the engaged Buddhist movement has been the lack of an effective means of communication and cooperation. To this end, the international Network of Engaged Buddhists has recently been formed to link concerned Buddhist and relevant non-Buddhist organizations and individuals. It will act as a clearinghouse of information on groups and activities and aid in the coordination of efforts wherever possible. The network is open to all parties involved in social actions, be it in women's issues, human rights, peace work, alternative education, the environment, spiritual training, alternative economics, rural development, communications, or family concerns. They will also be involved in running courses in spirituality and meditation for activists.

SPIRITUALITY IN ACTIVISM

All religions contain an inherent tradition of social concern; thus, one is encouraged to become involved in society and not simply seek personal liberation. The message of the importance of social action in spirituality is fairly obvious.

It might be helpful to talk briefly about the other side of that argument — the importance of spirituality in social action. Certainly engaged Buddhists would agree with liberation theologians that the two should not be separated from each other.

For Buddhists, meditation is particularly important for maintaining awareness, both outwardly and inwardly. On this subject, Thich Nhat Hanh preaches, "Do not lose yourself in dispersion and in your surroundings. Learn to practice breathing in order to regain composure of the body and mind, to practice mindfulness, and to develop true concentration and understanding."[9] This may be something that Buddhists can share and participate in with people from other religious backgrounds.

Indeed, internal and external development must take place at the same time if we are to be effective and constructive in our work. Each person must strive to find and keep their balance. Once one becomes aware of one's own ego and discovers the fallacy of it, one becomes less emotionally invested and more able to do what compassion requires. When we try to change our external world without training our mind to be calm and selfless, it becomes difficult to see things the way they really are, and thus it is impossible to carry out our tasks objectively. On working without developing mindfulness, Ken Jones has written:

> Dedication to a great cause can give meaning to life and a heart-warming sense of righteousness and group solidarity, even though these gratifications may filter out a lot of reality. Similarly, doing good to other people can make me feel good at the expense of undermining their dignity and autonomy.[10]

Yet, Buddhists are discouraged from paying uncritical respect to the Buddha's words. Cultivating blind attachment to any ideology on a collective level can be extremely dangerous. Thich Nhat Hanh says, "Do not be idolatrous or bound to any doctrine, theory or ideology, even Buddhist ones. All systems of thought are guiding means; they are not absolute truth. . . . If you have a gun, you can shoot one, two, three, five people, but if you have an ideology and stick to it, thinking it is the absolute truth, you can kill millions. . . . Peace can only be achieved when we are not attached to a view, when we are free from fanaticism."[11]

It is in this context that spirituality is important in social action—"as a guiding means." With critical self-awareness, we can genuinely understand and respect others of various religions and beliefs.

Our common enemies are consumerism, oppression, and militarism. Buddhists and Christians should join hands in working for peace and social justice, and in liberating themselves from our geocentricity, selfishness, and intolerance, so that we can act as normal people without fear, insecurity, or feelings of superiority or inferiority. It is important to realize that many of the divergences existing among religions are often complementary visions, which should not be seen as conflictual, but rather as differences which lead to deeper, more universal positions through a process of dialogue. It is crucial, then, that this process is guaranteed to take place by the religions, their institutions, and by society and the state.

In response to Deane Ferm's "clarion call" at the end of the opening chapter, it is my view that people of different religious backgrounds not only can, but must, work together. It is not enough to look back to the essential teachings of our own heritage; we must find good friends beyond our religious affiliations if we are to achieve true liberation, justice, and peace.

In closing, perhaps a quote from the Dalai Lama seems most appropriate:

> Today we have become so interdependent and so closely connected with each other that without a sense of universal responsibility, irrespective of different ideologies and faiths, our very existence or survival would be difficult.

NOTES

1. Ken Jones, *Buddhism and Social Action* (Kandy, Sri Lanka: Buddhist Publication Society, 1981).

2. Buddhadasa Bhikku, *Dhammic Socialism* (Bangkok: Thai Interreligious Commission for Development, 1986).

3. Ken Jones, *Buddhism and Social Action.*

4. David Brandon, *Zen and the Art of Helping* (London: Routledge and Kegan Paul, 1976).

5. Prayudh Payutto, *Freedom: Individual and Social* (Bangkok, 1987).

6. Walpola Rahula, *Zen and the Taming of the Bull: Essays* (Gordon Fraser, 1978).

7. E.F. Schumacher, *Small Is Beautiful: Economics as if Human Beings Mattered* (Blond and Briggs, 1973).

8. Buddhadasa Bhikku, *Dhammic Socialism.*

9. Thich Nhat Hahn, *Being Peace* (Berkeley, CA: Parallax Press).

10. Ken Jones, *Buddhism and Social Action.*

11. Thich Nhat Hahn, *Being Peace.*

6

Out of Africa

African Traditional Religion and African Theology

JOSIAH U. YOUNG III

In this essay, I will discuss the relation of African traditional religion to liberation theology. I undertake this analysis as an African-American whose work focuses on African theology, Black theology and African traditional religion.[1]

Liberation theology is a recent development of Christian consciousness that asserts God's partiality to the oppressed. Liberation theology includes Latin American, Asian, Black North American, and African theologies, each of which is uniquely suited to its context, but all of which are linked to one another in a preferential option for the poor. I focus primarily on African theology when discussing liberation theology as it emerges from the context from which African traditional religion emerges.

African traditional religion of Black Africa, on the other hand, is neither Christian nor Muslim. Rather it is a religion that indicates the living memory of ancestral values and may be discussed in terms of the visible and the invisible. The visible signifies human beings, flora, fauna, and the artifacts, insignia, and mnemonic utterances that connote the symbols of a localized cosmos.[2] The visible is the natural and cultural environment, of which humans, always in the process of transformation, are at the center. The invisible connotes the numinous field of ancestors, spirits, divinities, and the Supreme Being, all of whom, in varying degrees, permeate the visible. Visible things, however, are not always what they seem. Pools, rocks, flora, and fauna may dissimulate invisible forces of which only the initiated are conscious.

African traditional religion constitutes as many nuances of meanings as there are distinct Black African people. It would seem, then, that one would write of African tradition religions. I use the singular term because of the view, held particularly by African theologians, that the traditional religions of Black Africa are similar enough to talk of African traditional religion in a generic sense, the danger of reification notwithstanding.[3] In order to mitigate reification, I will generally refer in this essay to the Yoruba of Nigeria. I have chosen these people because their legacies are clearly part of the cultural memory of African-Americans, a community to which I belong.[4] Attention is also given to the traditional Bakongo (Zaire), Fon (Dahomey = Benin), Senufo (Burkino Faso), Akan (Ghana) and the Luo (Kenya).

I discuss African theology in terms of the new and old guards.[5] The new guard are liberation theologians for whom inculturation is inextricable from the quests to liberate the African poor from the socioeconomic problems of Africa.[6] Inculturation entails the process by which Christianity changes traditional culture and yet becomes a part of that culture.[7] Indispensable to their discussions regarding inculturation is an appreciation of African traditional religion.

The old guard, on the other hand, are not liberation theologians, but theologians of indigenization, that is, they tend to focus exclusively on the process of inculturation. Socioeconomic problems, which indicate the need for liberation in the wake of independence, have not been the essential concern of the old guard. Nonetheless, study of the old guard is indispensable in that they have identified continuities between African traditional religion and Christianity, thereby facilitating the work of the new guard.

My discussion of the relation of African traditional religion to African theology is structured by examination of social analysis, praxis, religiocultural analysis, hermeneutics, God, sin, and salvation. In my discussion of these elements, I focus on the differences and similarities between African traditional religion and African theology as a liberation theology.

DIFFERENCES

SOCIAL ANALYSIS

A fundamental difference between African traditional religion and African theology may be discussed in terms of social analysis, which Clodovis and Leonardo Boff call "socio-analytical mediation."[8] Social analysis is an essential element of liberation theology, because it identifies the material and ideological determinants which oppress the poor. Social analysis, moreover, is critical for praxis—revolutionary activity that involves the tension between theory and practice. In liberation theology, social analysis is informed by socialist theories that facilitate decisions as to what must be done to change oppressive contexts into liberating ones.

In the new guard's theology, social analysis identifies class contradictions in terms of hierarchical stratifications in which the oppressed peasant and workers are at the bottom and the African bourgeoisie at the top. Social analysis reveals a neocolonial structure that perpetuates the underdevelopment of the African poor to the profit of the capitalist West.[9]

African traditional religion offers no counterpart to African theology in terms of social analysis. In African traditional religion, socioeconomic contradictions are not identified for the sake of revolutionary change. Rather, focus has been on the maintenance of the social system that includes relationships between the living and the dead as well as political organizations and modes of economic reproduction. The maintenance of the social system involves the re-creation of sacred time which, according to Mircea Eliade, "is a primordial mythical time made present."[10]

Among the Yoruba, mythical time is made present in rituals. One ritual is that of the Egun-gun cult, in which the initiated dress in masked costumes that symbolize the return of the dead. The Egun-gun ritual maintains the social order under the auspices of the ancestors and renews an appreciation of the deep wells of community. Other rituals that involve specific *òrìsà*(s) (divinities) such as Shango or Ogun also enforce social order.[11] Rituals involve liminality.[12] Liminality "is an experience of temporary loss of status and social distinctions in which the deep springs of human relatedness are rediscovered."[13] Among the Bakongo, mythical time is made present in the drawing of the traditional cosmogram, *yowa*, and the swearing of the oath that invites the judgment of the ultimate.[14] The cosmogram, which is the insignia of the perpetual complementarity of the visible and the invisible, valorizes the social order.[15]

Clearly, then, the social analysis undertaken by African theologians signifies a matrix of social relationships quite different from that of the traditional world views of the Bakongo and the Yoruba. African theologians recognize this difference in their respect of African traditional religion. Jean-Marc Éla put it this way:

> The African traditions may seem to act as a brake on social changes, but in reality it is an awareness of their identity that black peasants find their reasons for rejecting a developmental model that generates economic surplus to be divided up by foreign capitalists and local bureaucracies. Their religious life has ever enabled African peoples to fight foreign economic, political, and cultural domination.[16]

While Éla valorizes the autonomy of African traditional religion, his appropriation of that religion is a component of social analysis, which differs from what devotees of African traditional religion are doing in terms of their symbols and rituals.

What Éla reveals, however, is that African traditional religion is not retrogressive when compared to liberation theology that focuses on societal transformation. African traditional religion is not an old relic giving way to the dynamism of African theology. Despite, for instance, the neocolonial realities of Nigeria, Yoruba religion still abides with great ancestral intensity. The priest-diviner, the *babalawo*, is still well-respected, and the *òrìsà(s)*, the divinities, continue to reveal in possession trance the closeness and the usefulness of the invisible forces of healing and wholeness. Among the Bakongo of Zaire, the traditional sense of the complementarity of the visible and the invisible continues to give meaning to neocolonial life, though traditional Bakongo religion has been modified by neocolonial crises. In short, the ancestral values of African people persist. Adapted to neocolonial realities and interpreted according to traditional sensibilities, they are rich in liberating values.[17]

PRAXIS

Praxis also reflects a significant difference between liberation theology and African traditional religion. Praxis indicates an activism which seeks to change oppressive contexts into ones that are humane. As Gustavo Gutiérrez proclaims, liberation theologies are epiphenomenal to human commitments to societal transformation.[18] This is not to suggest that faith is secondary to the liberation struggle. New guard theologian Jean-Marc Éla, puts it this way:

> Faith is the demand for an incarnation of the gospel in a society undergoing radical transformations. Faith is experienced, in living fashion, in an awareness of a human being to invent and a world to build. Faith is the engagement of a community of women and men who, in the very act of looking to Jesus as a group, feel responsible for the gospel ... In short, faith is verified and actualized wherever the future is striven for and invented, in all of society's tension spots. Unless it takes account of economics as well as the realities of power and the correlative realities of powerlessness, faith is disincarnate.[19]

Valorization of praxis does not identify the anticipated transformed context with the Kingdom of God. The Kingdom of God signifies ultimate liberation—the promise of transhistorical "life" which ends all struggle. Fundamental to praxis, then, are eschatological values that signify that revolutionary praxes are penultimate orientations. Eschatological values are intrinsic to the faith of African theologians. Faith manifests the grace of Christ essentially responsible for the commitment to praxis.

Faith often indicates a trinitarian structure, found in the works of African theologians such as Mercy Oduyoye.[20] Central to faith is the personal assurance of salvation in Christ, which is imparted by the Spirit. Thus Christ and the Spirit, truly God from the "Father," are close to human beings in a way definitive for an understanding of the soteriological connotations of "faith" and praxis.

Faith, understood in terms of ecclesial dogmas, has no counterpart in African traditional religion. Michael Kirwen, the Maryknoll missioner who has recorded his dialogue with a Luo diviner, reveals: "The very words used by African Christians to express such doctrines such as the Trinity seem to have a life of their own and are continually used in contexts that have no meaning."[21]

Praxis, however, is not, in its widest implication, alien to traditional African sensibility. Of course, I speak here of a "praxis" radically different from that defined in African theology. In general, insofar as ritual signifies the doing of religion, it may be said to constitute a form of "praxis." The "praxis" of traditional religion, we are to understand, regulates the cosmos. This "praxis" involves divination and sacrifice, invocation and possession trance. Africans are edified in their religion as they effect it in ritual.[22]

African traditional religion, in addition, reveals that violence, an element of praxis, is an acceptable means of repelling intruders or of attempting to settle conflicts. Indeed, the wars of the Zulu and the Asante against the British reveal that African traditional religion has not eschewed violence. Traditional violence here, however, emerged from an animus inextricable from a structure defined by ancestral modalities. The revolutionary violence that promotes change and is accepted by certain African theologians is related to socialist paradigms.[23] (This does not mean that traditional Zulu values are less revolutionary than Marxist ones.)

The violence of the Dahomean Amazons, the civil wars of the Yoruba, and their wars with Dahomey in the nineteenth century, though, have no real relation to liberation. That traditional violence fed the slave trade.[24] The Maji-Maji rebellion of East Africa during the early part of the twentieth century, however—as well as the revolutionary violence of devotees to African religion in the Diaspora—reveals the way in which African traditional religion condones violence in a way relevant to liberation theology.[25]

One can also look at the legacy of the Mau-Mau rebellion. Within the olden colonial context of Kenya, the Mau-Mau violently resisted the hegemony of the British settlers. Mau-Mau—perhaps a corruption of the Kikuyu word for oath, *muma*—was based upon the traditional Kikuyu sense of the sacredness of their ancestral land.[26] The revolutionary theorist and "general," Amilcar Cabral—particularly given his definition of re-Africanization—also indicates how violence, understood in relation to traditional mores, can be liberating.[27]

RELIGIO-CULTURAL ANALYSIS

Differences between African traditional religion and African theology may be explored further in terms of religio-cultural analysis. Religio-cultural analysis is a critical epistemic element in the liberation theologies of the Ecumenical Association of Third World Theologians as well as the Ecumenical Association of African Theologians.[28] In terms of religio-cultural analysis, Asian theologian Aloysius Pieris explains that no

> true liberation is possible unless persons are "religiously motivated" toward it . . . the peoples of the Third World will not spontaneously embark on a costly adventure unless their lives are touched and their depths stirred by its prospects along the "cultural" patterns of their own "religious histories."[29]

Religio-cultural analysis, then, entails appreciation of popular culture. According to Latin American theologian Enrique Dussel, popular culture

> preserves the best of the Third World and is the one whence new alternatives will emerge for future world culture, which will not be a mere replication of the structures of the center. The exteriority of popular culture is the best guarantee and the least contaminated nucleus of the new humankind. Its values, scorned today . . . must be studied carefully; they must be augmented within a new pedagogy of the oppressed. It is within popular culture, even traditional culture, that cultural revolution will find its most authentic content.[30]

As Dussel reveals, religio-cultural analysis uncovers the values of the oppressed in the realization that these values, often non-Christian, constitute the modalities which resist the oppressor. Indeed—as I have noted—the late African revolutionary, Amilcar Cabral, explains that African peasants' consciousness of the modern contradictions that subjugate them is first expressed in their assertion of their cultural difference from the oppressor.[31] Indeed, the political implications of religio-cultural analysis impel new guard theologians, such as Mercy Oduyoye, to study African traditional religion precisely because this religion constitutes much of the world view of the African oppressed.

In African theology, moreover, religio-cultural analysis signifies the reciprocity of inculturation and acculturation. Mercy Oduyoye explains the reciprocity in terms of a critical distinction:

> Acculturation [is] used to refer to the efforts of Africans to use things African in their practice of Christianity, inculturation as the manifestation of changes that have come into the African way of life a result of the Christian faith.[32]

Without acculturation, Christian theology is not African; without inculturation, African theology is not Christian.

An outstanding example of the way in which acculturation and inculturation work together to produce an African liberation theology is Jean-Marc Éla's vision of eucharist rooted in the soil of the Kirdi of North Cameroon. He argues that it would be far more appropriate to use millet and nut beer rather than the imported wine and wafers which the Kirdi do not cultivate and which have no meaning in the subsistence economy of their ancestors.[33] "When all is said and done," asks Éla, "what answer can be made to people who ask, Why say Mass with those little white things when millet means so much to us?"[34]

Still, an African theology that valorizes religio-cultural analysis is quite different from the African traditional religion studied by the theologian. That is not to say that African traditional religion is without religio-cultural analysis.

Priest-diviners, such as the *babalawos* of Yoruba religion, engage in a religio-cultural analysis revelatory of a traditional African "praxis" and essentially unrelated to theories of acculturation and inculturation.[35] *Babalawos*, in service of the *òrìsà* Orunmila (also known as Ifa), diagnose clients' problems and prescribe remedies for them based on the correspondence between the pattern of divining elements, such as palm nuts, and a corpus of verses called *odu*, which *babalawos* have memorized.[36]

In fact, according to William Bascom, an authority on Yoruba religion, a *babalawo* memorizes over a thousand *odu*.[37] One such verse might be the following:

"Forest is the forest of fire" and "Grassland is the land of the sun" were the ones who cast Ifa for Orunmila on the day that he went to bury medicine against abiku in a hole in a refuse heap. When Orunmila was troubled by abiku, he went to the diviners. "Forest is the forest of fire" and "Grassland is the grassland of the sun." They told him that he should make a sacrifice, and he sacrificed. From that time on, his wife stopped bearing abiku.

Ifa says that abiku are "fighting with" this person; if he is able to sacrifice, they will stop.[38]

Yoruba attribute individual misfortune to unpropitious acts or to dissatisfaction among elemental forces, all of which disrupt human relationships and thus the balance between the visible and the invisible. In this case, the *abiku* represent forces of the invisible who are dissatisfied. The *abiku* are children who are born only to die. In a sense, they are spirits who promote trouble as they exacerbate anxiety related to the unborn, who link the living and the dead, the sky and the earth. Sacrifice to the sacred forces of the invisible facilitates the *abiku's* "staying" and thus enables the succession of generations—the prolongation of the Yoruba.[39] Such succession is the normal state of things and contributes to the production of equilibrium within society.

The *odu* to which I have referred above recounts a mythic structure also indicative of sacred time.[40] In divining that the client's misfortune is related to the *abiku*, the *babalawo* re-creates sacred time in reenacting the original encounter between Orunmila — a theophany of the sacred — and the ancestral *babalawos*.

In Yoruba religion, "religio-cultural analysis" reflects traditional belief in the visible matrix of a localized cosmos — that is, the topology and taxonomy defined by a Yoruba kingdom. At the center of this matrix are human beings whom òrìsà(s) possess in order to enforce morality and prescribe remedies for healing and wholeness.

"Religio-cultural analysis" in Yoruba religion is structured by the quest to bring opposite forces into equilibrium and symmetry. Opposite forces, signified by the leitmotifs, the visible and the invisible, are integrated in myth and in ritual in order to valorize their proportion in relation to one another. The opposition between the sky and the earth, man and woman, east and west, village and forest, culture and nature, constitutes cosmological poetics[41] which is polyrhythmic and polyphonic.

It bears repeating that religio-cultural analysis, confined to the boundaries of traditional religion, is part of a structure unrelated to attempts to lay epistemological foundations for an African theology concerned with the problem of inculturation — the relation of a Jewish and Christian God to Black African ancestral values. Indeed, more essential than God to the religio-cultural analysis of African traditional religion are the ancestors.

Even if one attempts to relate the ancestors to the *sanctorum communio*, he or she is basically making a heuristic point, albeit one which valorizes the indispensability of religio-cultural analysis in African theology. An eschatological world view signified by the *sanctorum communio* differs radically from a world view in which the earth is the locus of spiritual aspiration.

African theology is this-worldly, but conveys, as I have noted, the promise of transhistorical life with God. The struggle for liberation is a penultimate struggle, en route to and corrected daily by the proleptic reality of the Kingdom of God. The traditional African, however, is stubbornly earthbound, determined in many cases to return to the earth in someone or something.[42] For the most part, the African does not hope for eternal life in the "good heaven." Yoruba religion may seem to be an exception in this regard, for when souls have lived virtuously, they reach "good heaven" (*orun rere*).[43] Yoruba souls, however, desire fervently to return to earth. Thus, "heaven" is the quintessential reward, precisely because it is the mode which facilitates reincarnation.

Traditional Africans are rooted in the earth in part because of the way in which they recognize distinctions between God and humankind. The Luo diviner, Riana, explains that

to live once again with God is foreign to our way of thinking. We have such a respect and image of God that we cannot conceive of living with or sharing in divine life and power ... No, what God has given us is sufficient. We are only human, and we shall remain as such. God is indeed the God of humankind—but God is also God.[44]

HERMENEUTICS

Yet another difference between African traditional religion and African theology may be discussed in terms of what Clodovis and Leonardo Boff call hermeneutical mediation. In liberation theology, religio-cultural and social analysis form axes of a hermeneutical circle in which Scripture and tradition are reinterpreted in ways that are liberating.[45] In African theology, hermeneutical mediation produces African interpretations of Scripture and tradition that challenge eurocentric theology. Jean-Marc Éla puts it this way:

If Christianity wants to reach Africans, to speak to their hearts, and to enter their consciousness and the space where their soul breathes, it must change. To do so, Christianity must do violence to itself and break the chains of western rationality, which means almost nothing in the African civilization of the symbol. Without some form of epistemological break with the scholastic universe, Christianity has little chance of reaching the African.[46]

The epistemological break facilitates an African rereading of Scripture, in part because it is informed by the symbolism of African traditional religion. In African traditional religion, however, we find no hermeneutical circle. In African traditional religion, the Bible is not the text emblematic of religious values. As I have noted above, the texts of African traditional religion are the insignia and artifacts related to divination, which is part of the dialectic of myth and ritual. It is not unlikely, however, that the Bible may be incorporated into traditional religion. The incorporation, however, would have little to do with a hermeneutical understanding of the West, but rather an understanding inextricable from traditional values.

SIMILARITIES

Much attention had been given to differences between African traditional religion and African theology. There are, however, similarities between the two that have been identified by African theologians, particularly the old guard. It bears repeating that, while the old guard are not liberation theologians, their pioneering work is a foundation on which new guard theologians continue to build.[47] In terms of systematic theology, the old guard has juxtaposed select dimensions of African traditional religion and Christian doctrine. For example, the old guard abstracted from specific ethnic groups traditional aspects that appeared to fit under certain doctrinal headings such as God, sin, and salvation.[48]

In discussing similarities between African theology and African traditional religion, then, I will focus on those doctrinal headings. My discussion by no means reflects all that may be said of the similarities. In discussing similarities, however, I must continue to highlight differences. Not to discuss similarity in terms of dissimilarity will distort not only African traditional religion, but African theology as well. Thus, my discussion is in terms of similarity in difference. This principle, similarity in difference, is based on the realization that the closer one looks at the similarities, the more dissimilarities come to the fore. I turn now to a discussion of God.

GOD

Appealing to a view of general revelation, African theologians such as John Mbiti, Bolaji Idowu, and John Pobee have claimed that Africans have traditionally believed in a Supreme Being who is essentially the Jewish and Christian God.[49] Their view is traceable to Wilhelm Schmidt, a German missionary who worked among the Pygmies of Central Africa. Schmidt subscribed to the view that a perception of the one God was of necessity present in the context of "primitive religion."[50] Schmidt thought that "primitive religion" was initially monotheistic, though he claimed that it later degenerated into polytheism. His position has served as an epistemological foundation of much of the Christian scholarship on African concepts of God and has helped to establish the view that there are similarities between Christianity and African traditional religion.[51]

Mbiti put it this way:

> There are serious missionary writers who have admitted or acknowledged that African Religion is talking about the one and same God as the Bible. For example John V. Taylor in his *The Primal Vision* . . . acknowledges that Africa has known God all these millennia. Another major missionary contributor to this debate was Edwin W. Smith who held the opinion that the same God is at work in the Judeo-Christian tradition and African religion.[52]

Here, Mbiti reproduces the methodology of missionaries who did not bracket their Christian self-understanding when interpreting African traditional religion.[53] Missionaries have assumed that one could assess the value of African traditional religion in terms of Christianity.

African traditional religionists, however, mean something quite different from African theologians when they speak of God, though both agree that there is a Supreme Being.

It is one thing to take traditional doctrines of God—God's moral attributes, God's intrinsic attributes, and the providence and sustenance of

God — and impose them on autochthonous conceptions of God.[54] It is quite another to deal with African conceptions of God in their autonomous integrity.

While the distance between God and humankind, within African traditional religion, increases the need of God, the renewal of the cosmos is in the hands of humankind whose knowledge of the visible and the invisible facilitates reincarnation. Reincarnation, in whatever form, is related to God in that God has instituted the cosmos in such a way that the ancestors and other intermediaries are accessible for the sake of the survival of the human genus. Riana, a Luo diviner, explains that "God [kiteme] is not remote from humanity. God created lesser deities . . . to watch over and care for humanity."[55]

Among the Yoruba, God (Olodumare) watches over and cares for humanity through the *òrìsà*(s) who are summoned by priests and other devotees who serve an *òrìsà*. *Òrìsà*(s) are very anthropomorphic and may be deified ancestors or assume the personality of an outstanding member of a cult. An *òrìsà* is revealed during possession trance in rhythms and dances peculiar to him or her. Symbolized by certain colors and specific foods, an *òrìsà* is also associated with natural dimensions: thunder, the sky, rivers, the forests, smallpox, iron and paleolithic artifacts. These divinities enforce morality by punishing those who disrupt community. Although God — diffused in the divinities — is not remote, the closeness of God has little to do with a liberating Christian understanding of the closeness of God in Jesus. In the context of the traditional Luo, the diviner Riana put it this way:

> How can God be part of his own creation? Do not your teachings about Jesus dilute the true nature of God by bringing God physically into the world of humanity? Are you trying to say that God was also born a human being who was born, ate, slept, suffered, got sick, and died? But what is your point? What does this add to our understanding of God?[56]

The African God is not simultaneously human.

Neither is the African God creator in every case. Among the Yoruba, for instance, that role is associated with the *òrìsà* Obatala (king of white cloth). According to Yoruba myth:

> Obatala is the creator of man. Obatala made man out of clay. He molded men and women and he asked Olodumare to put the breath of life into them.[57]

After formation, Olodumare bestows the essential soul (*ori*) and breathes into the formed creature the breath of life.

The Fon of old Dahomey,[58] very much related to the Yoruba, also reveal that concepts of God in traditional religion may in specific instances mean something entirely different from God in the West. The Fon God (Nana Buluku) is a composite of both sexes. Indeed, among certain African people, God traditionally has had a male and female part, a view very much related to the traditional African valorization of androgyny as the ideal state.[59] This view is also found among the Senufo, who understand God in part as Ancient Mother.[60] The God of liberation theologians, however, is the God of Exodus who is revealed in Jesus. Liberation theologians have not generally thought of God as an androgynous being, though there are exceptions to this.[61] This distinction between conceptions of God held by liberation theologians and the Fon and Senufo reveals again that similarity is limited by difference.

SIN

According to John Mbiti:

Many scholars of African Religion recognize that what we call Sin has first and foremost to do with relationships in the community. In the African framework the community consists of the departed, the living and those yet to be born. Any breach which punctuates this communal relationship amounts to Sin, whatever may be used for this concept.[62]

Like liberation theologians, African traditional religionists hold that malignant antisocial acts destroy human community. For both, evil is not only to be found in an individual's heart but also in the social structures of society.

In African traditional religion, acts which disrupt traditional life cause misfortune. Failure to propitiate the ancestors, theft, incest, witchcraft— all are malignant acts that can cause death, disease, infertility, drought, and famine.

Thus J. Omosade Awolalu, in his seminal essay "Sin and its Removal," writes:

Sin is, therefore, doing that which is contrary to the will and directions of Deity. It [sin] includes any immoral behavior, ritual mistakes, any breach against God or man, breach of covenant, breaking of taboos, and doing anything as abominable and polluting. We cannot speak of Sin in isolation—it has got to be related to God and to man.[63]

Traditional concepts of communal infractions could very well be Christianized under the concept of sin. It is important to point out, however, that sin for liberation theologians signifies a fall from grace that is restored by God in the sacrifice of Christ on the cross. Humans can not save themselves apart from the salvation wrought in the crucifixion of the God-man, Jesus Christ.

In African traditional religion, what might be called a fall is not really a fall in the Jewish and Christian sense. Although African myths recount a primordial separation of God and humankind, which in many cases introduced death, these myths do not signify the total depravity of humankind. Indeed, Mbiti says as much:

> The separation between God and man was an ontological and not a moral separation. Man did not become a sinner by nature through these acts which brought about the loss of the primeval paradise. There is no original Sin in African Religion, neither is a person born a sinner. Man is a sinner by deed in the context of the community of which the person is a member.[64]

It bears repeating, however, that African traditional religionists believe that they, through sacrifice, have the power to correct broken relationships. Sacrifice appeases the forces of the invisible, particularly the ancestors who enforce the morality taught in the sacred time of the beginning. Diviners, in reading the indices of the cosmos, determine which sacrifice will purge witchcraft or appease ancestors responsible for communal stress. A single Savior through whom all is made right once and for all — especially for those with the gift of faith — is foreign to the traditional African sensibility.

That Jesus is immolated to restore an element of sacred time is nonetheless similar to the function of sacrifice in African traditional religion. Sacrifice essentially restores communal equilibrium in correcting "sin," thereby putting everything in its place. Similarly, Jesus' immolation signifies the mitigation of sin and the restoration of broken relationships.

SALVATION

Mbiti claims that "within the African religio-cultural setting ... the terms for Salvation seem to indicate ... the physical welfare of life."[65] For Mbiti, the traditional concern for the well-being of persons is not unlike a salvific Christian concern for the welfare of life. Indeed, soteriology in African theology signifies a penultimate orientation in which redemption indicates the well-being of human beings. This redemptive structure is essentially established by Christ. "The saving activities in African Religion," writes Mbiti, "belong to the more cosmic saving activities of God. They are related to the ultimate Salvation brought about by God through Jesus Christ."[66]

In African traditional religion, however, "salvation" is not related to Christ, but to rituals which seek to promote fertility, fecundity, healing, and other modes of being emblematic of cosmological harmony. As I have noted above, traditional rituals valorize the earth in a way distinct from the eschatological self-understanding of liberation theologians. Thus, conversion of the heart or individual enlightenment, which signify christological and pneumatological values, are not sufficient to remove evil and suffering. What is needed is the diviner's identification of the source of trouble and prescription for the mode of sacrifice which would dissolve the impediment.

While one might say that a traditional diviner would agree with liberation theologians that salvation is not really possible unless there is a transformation of this world, the diviner's understanding of "salvation" is radically different. In the words of Michael Kirwen, a Maryknoll priest and interpreter of African traditional religion, the diviner sees

> no moral separation of humankind and God, salvation must be in terms of the here and now. He thinks of "everlasting life" in terms of the possibility of somehow returning through reincarnation to this world as a human being. It is in this context that the whole scenario of grandchildren being the returned ancestors makes sense. Life for [the diviner] is a continuum embracing the dead, the unborn, and the living. This belief promotes the solidarity of the living and the dead in a way unheard of in Western thought.[67]

Unlike the liberation theologian, the diviner does not understand transformation in terms of the ultimacy of the New Creation, a creation infinitely different from what has been known by humankind. Rather, transformation for the diviner signifies a metamorphosis inextricable from this world, a metamorphosis in which humans return in some form to the earth.

Similarities between African traditional religion and a liberating Christianity have, indeed, facilitated African theologians' attempts to make theology relevant to the life and thought of African people. Indeed, the analogy between Christianity and African traditional religion promises new vistas in theological method. One can see this promise in African independent churches where startlingly vibrant expressions of African Christianity well from the richness of ancestral religions.

CONCLUSION

African theologians, such as Mercy Oduyoye, Jean-Marc Éla, Barthélemy Adoukonou, and Englebert Mveng, know that the religion of the peasants has much to teach them regarding the meaning of liberation in Africa. Indeed, other liberation theologians can learn much from these peasants, who still cherish the virtues of their ancestors. From the Africans, liberation theologians learn that an oppressed people who do not valorize their ancestors or apply the insights of tradition to the struggle for liberation are neither wise nor prudent. Memories of the ancestors—that is, the villagers who have sacrificed their lives in the struggles for independence—

are particularly relevant for an African theology in touch with the meaning of liberation.[68]

African traditional religion can also sensitize liberation theologians to the necessity to respect the "livingness" of the environment. Indeed, the ancestors remind us that the earth is our home, and the prolongation of humankind is intimately bound to the earth's fecundity. The sky, the earth, and all the living and breathing things that give life and balance to the cosmos are essential to the quest for the new humanity (*Fanon*). And so, the ancestors teach us that that we must listen to this earth, feel its pulse, if we are to recognize our connection to the sacred. African traditional religion reminds liberation theologians of the sacredness of the invisible — the reality of the sacred and the involvement of divinity in all that pertains to health and wholeness.

Just as African theologians of liberation are enriched by their traditional religions, African traditional religionists are enriched by the insights of liberation theologians. In making a preferential option for the poor, African theologians are helping to move peasants to a consciousness through which

> they break the bonds of the village universe to integrate progressively into the country and the world; . . . acquire . . . new knowledge, useful for their immediate and future activity within the framework of the struggle, and . . . strengthen their political awareness by assimilating the principles of national and social revolution postulated by the struggle. They thereby become more able to play the decisive role of providing the principle force behind the liberation movement.[69]

African theologians are indispensable to the poor in explaining to them the praxis best suited for the quest for liberation. Indeed, despite their religious differences, both African theologians and African religionists recognize the need to deal with the oppressive problems of neocolonial Africa. The African theologian's scientific analysis of the socioeconomic contradictions of oppressive societies is useful to the peasants who need to discover the most effective courses of action.

It is likely, then, that the African theologian and the traditional diviner, because of their common experiences of oppression, can work shoulder to shoulder — *dans une coude a coude fraternel*[70] — in the struggle to end oppression.

NOTES

1. See my *Black and African Theologies: Siblings or Distant Cousins?* (Maryknoll, N.Y.: Orbis Books, 1986).

2. See Jean-Marc Éla, *My Faith as an African* (Maryknoll, N.Y.: Orbis Books, 1988). He writes that "the African civilization is a civilization of symbols. In it relationships between one human being and another, and between human beings

and nature pass through the invisible, the symbolic place where all reality acquires meaning. Then the truly real is invisible and the visible only appearance — all is symbol. Africans live then in a 'forest of symbols,' a unique way of maintaining their relationships to the universe" (p. 35).

3. See Bolaji Idowu, *African Traditional Religion: A Definition* (Maryknoll, N.Y.: Orbis Books, 1975).

4. See Bastide, *The African Religions of Brazil: Toward a Sociology of the Interpretation of Civilizations* (Baltimore: The Johns Hopkins University Press, 1978); and Robert Ferris Thompson, *Flash of the Spirit* (New York: Vintage Books, 1984).

5. See my "African Theology: From 'Independence' Toward Liberation," *Voices From The Third World* 10 (1987).

6. Ibid., pp. 44–47.

7. See Aylward Shorter, *Toward a Theology of Inculturation* (Maryknoll, N.Y.: Orbis Books, 1988).

8. Leonardo and Clodovis Boff, *Introducing Liberation Theology* (Maryknoll, N.Y.: Orbis Books, 1987), pp. 24–32.

9. A paradigm of this social analysis is found in Jean-Marc Éla, *African Cry* (Maryknoll, N.Y.: Orbis Books, 1986). Éla's social analysis focuses on the illusion of independence and the perniciousness of neocolonialism, concluding that "after more than twenty years of experience with democracy African style, for many, the situation is worse than it was before" (p. 137). See also his *L'Afrique des villages* (Paris: Editions Karthala, 1982); *La ville en Afrique noire* (Paris: Editions Karthala, 1983); "Luttes pour la santé de l'homme et royaume de Dieu dans l'Afrique d'aujourd'hui," *Bulletin de théologie africaine* 5 (January, June 1983): 65–84.

10. Mircea Eliade, *The Sacred and the Profane: The Nature of Religion* (New York: Harcourt Brace Jovanovich, 1959) p. 68.

11. Benjamin Ray, *African Religions: Symbol, Ritual, and Community* (Englewood Cliffs, N.J.: Prentice-Hall, 1976), p. 81.

12. See Evan M. Zuesse, *Ritual Cosmos: The Sanctification of Life in African Religions* (Ohio: Ohio University Press, 1979). According to Zuesse, liminality has two components "applicable throughout African religions: positive liminality, which integrates structures and builds up a divine order; and a negative liminality which destroys order and isolates its victims" (35). The Egun-gun signify a positive liminality. Witches who destroy order in devouring human souls signify a negative liminality. See also Victor Turner, " 'Betwixt and Between': The Liminal Period in Rites of Passage," in *The Forest of Symbols: Aspects of Ndembu Ritual* (Ithaca, N.Y.: Cornell University Press, 1989). According to Turner, the liminal is that spaceless, timeless plane on which the initiate, poised at the crossroads of stateless being (neither boy nor man), leaves that stateless void between boyhood and manhood and crosses over to the latter. "Betwixt and between" in that way, the liminal subject experiences with others a quintessential democracy or *communitas*.

13. John R. Hinnells, *A Handbook of Living Religions* (New York: Viking Penguin, 1987), p. 434.

14. See Robert Ferris Thompson, *Flash of the Spirit*, pp. 108–11; Wyatt MacGaffey, *Religion and Society in Central Africa: The BaKongo of Lower Zaire* (Chicago: The University of Chicago Press, 1986); and MacGaffey, *Modern Kongo Prophets: Religion in a Plural Society* (Bloomington: Indiana University Press, 1983).

15. Ibid.

16. Jean-Marc Éla, *African Cry*, pp. 45–46.

17. See Jean-Marc Éla, *My Faith as an African*. Éla writes that "great importance should be given to the cultural factors that inspired the initial resistance to foreign control. The supposition that the black world is incapable of popular mobilization is based on a naive vision of African reality. African forms of expression refute the supposed passivity or resignation of the black peoples in the face of glaring injustices. The seeds of struggle and resistance that correspond to the genius of these peoples are concealed everywhere" (p. xvi). Another new guard theologian, Barthélemy Adoukonou, makes a similar point, but with a focus on the revolutionary power of neo-African religion in the New World. See his *Jalons pour une théologie africaine. Essai d'une hermé neutique chrétienne du Vodun dahoméen. Tome I: Critique théologique* (Paris: Editions Lethielleux, 1980).

18. Gustavo Gutiérrez, *A Theology of Liberation* (Maryknoll, N.Y.: Orbis Books, 1988), p. xxxiii.

19. Jean-Marc Éla, *African Cry*, p. 91. See also his "Luttes pour la santé de l'homme et Royaume de Dieu dans l'Afrique d'aujourd'hui," *Bulletin de théologies africaine* 5, 9 (January, June 1983): pp. 74–84.

20. See Mercy Oduyoye, *Hearing and Knowing* (Maryknoll, N.Y.: Orbis Books, 1986), pp. 144–45.

21. Michael C. Kirwen, *The Missionary and the Diviner* (Maryknoll, N.Y.: Orbis Books, 1988), p. 23.

22. In the words of Evan Zuesse, ritual is the means by which "the whole of life can be sanctified ... African spirituality, above and beyond the specific focus of particular ritual actions, is always directed toward the sanctity of the universe as a whole. Every action on its deepest level seeks to sustain the divine order and its continual self-regeneration; in this sense every ritual enactment, however superficially orientated to utilitarian goals, is utterly selfless" (*Ritual Cosmos*, p. 242).

23. For an example of the ways in which African theologians accept violence, see Éla's *African Cry*, pp. 56–65. It is important to note that Éla does not subscribe to Marxist theory in this respect. His theorist is Frantz Fanon. Marxist values maybe seen in Buti Tlhagale, "On Violence: A Township Perspective," in Itumeleng J. Mosala and Buti Tlhagale, eds., *The Unquestionable Right to be Free: Black Theology From South Africa* (Maryknoll, N.Y.: Orbis Books, 1986), pp. 131–51.

24. Indeed, one of the great ancestors of African theology, Bishop Samuel Crowther, was as a boy sold into slavery as a result of the civil wars among the Yoruba. The African-American anthropologist Zora Neal Hurston recalls an ex-slave, Cudjoe Lewis, who had been sold into slavery after being captured by the fierce Dahomean women who sacked his village. On the Amazons of Dahomey, see Zora Neal Hurston, *Dust Tracks On a Road: An Autobiography* (Chicago: University of Illinois Press, 1984), pp. 200–202. See also Jean-Marc Éla, *L'Afrique des villages*. The violence to which Éla refers here is structural and precolonial.

25. See Benjamin Ray, *African Religions*, pp. 156–58; and Barthélemy Adoukonou, *Jalons pour une théologie africaine*, pp. 57–59.

26. Ibid., pp. 165–71.

27. See *Unity and Struggle: Speeches and Writings of Amilcar Cabral*, with introduction by Basil Davidson and biographical notes by Mario Andrade (New York: Monthly Review Press, 1979), p. 143.

28. For an excellent summary of the history and meaning of the Ecumenical Association of Third World Theologians, see James Cone, *For My People: Black Theology and the Black Church* (Maryknoll, N.Y.: Orbis Books, 1984), pp. 144–56.

See also Virginia Fabella and Sergio Torres, eds., *Irruption of The Third World: Challenge to Theology* (Maryknoll, N.Y.: Orbis Books, 1983). Regarding L'association oecuménique des théologiens africaines, see Englebert Mveng, "L'association oecuménique des théologiens africaines en l'an 100 des Eglises africaines," *Bulletin de théologie africaine* 3, 5 (January, June 1981); "Récent développements de la theologie africaine," *Bulletin de théologie africaine*, 5, 9 (January, June 1983): 137–44.

29. In Virginia Fabella and Sergio Torres, *Irruption of the Third World*, p. 127.

30. Enrique Dussel, *Philosophy of Liberation* (Maryknoll, N.Y.: Orbis Books, 1985), p. 90.

31. Africa Information Service, *Return to the Source: Selected Speeches of Amilcar Cabral* (New York: Monthly Review Press, 1973), p. 48.

32. Mercy Oduyoye, *Hearing and Knowing*, p. 69.

33. Jean-Marc Éla, *African Cry*, p. 4.

34. Ibid. See also A. Sanon, "L'humanité de l'Euchariste," *Bulletin de theologie africaine* 4, 7 (January, June 1982). Like Éla, Sanon asks, rhetorically, whether the point of the eucharist is to hold to a static representation of the elements. Although communion wafers and wine are thought by the West to be universal metaphors of flesh and blood, they do not fit the African context. According to Sanon, eucharistic elements should reflect the reality of the people. Christ transforms edible material — it does not really matter which — such that they become his body and blood, and thus Africans should use the more accessible grain (124). For Sanon, as for Éla, the edible substance is epiphenomenal to Christ who transforms the mundane thing into his body and blood. Salvation is not in zonfa or in millet and nut beer, or in the costly and imported wafers and wine, but in the will of Christ to eat with human beings, sharing the primordial conditions of ordinary life (127).

35. See Michael Kirwen, *The Missionary and the Diviner*. In *My Faith as an African*, Éla defines the traditional mode of religio-cultural analysis in terms of a "socio-cultural world where everything that happens has an inner meaning which must be deciphered . . . The events of daily life always have a meaning related to belief in the ancestors. Therefore reality must be 'decoded', starting with the different signs that manifest it" (p. 24).

36. William Bascom, *The Yoruba of Southwestern Nigeria* (Illinois: Waveland Press, 1969), p. 70.

37. Ibid., pp. 70–71.

38. William Bascom, *Ifa Divination: Communication Between Gods and Men in West Africa* (Bloomington: Indiana University Press, 1969), pp. 145–47.

39. William Bascom, *The Yoruba of Southwestern Nigeria*, p. 74.

40. According to Eliade, "myth shows how a reality came into existence, whether it be the total reality, the cosmos, or only a fragment — an island, a species of plant, a human institution. To tell how things came into existence is to explain them and at the same time indirectly answer another question: why did they come into existence? The why is explained in the how. To tell how a thing was born is to reveal an irruption of the sacred into the world, and the sacred is the ultimate cause of all real existence" (p. 97).

41. I choose the word "poetics" after being edified by Englebert Mveng's discussion of the difference between aesthetics and poetics in his seminal *L'art d'Afrique noire: liturgie cosmique et langage religieux* (Yaoun: Editions CLE, 1974). The text is a pioneering essay in religio-cultural analysis. He writes: "La Poétique Ban-

tou, nous entendons par là les lois du génie créateur de notre culture, ne peut donc en aucune façon être une esthétique. L'esthétique traduit la passivité du système sensoriel de l'homme devant le réel construit en spectacle et servi en nourriture pour sa concupiscence. La poétique, elle, se situe au moment où la spontanéité de l'homme se dresse contre le déterminisme de la nature et se constitue en liberté" (94). Thus the active spontaneity of poetics — a mode of religious discourse not unlike the improvisation one finds among jazz musicians of the Diaspora — is an ancestral mode of liberation.

42. See Dominique Zahan, *The Religion, Spirituality, and Thought of Traditional Africa* (Chicago: The University of Chicago Press, 1979), p. 155.

43. See William Bascom, pp. 75–76.

44. Michael Kirwen, *The Missionary and the Diviner*, p. 19.

45. See Juan Luis Segundo, *The Liberation of Theology* (Maryknoll, N.Y.: Orbis Books, 1975).

46. Jean-Marc Éla, *My Faith As An African*, p. 41.

47. See, for instance, Jean-Marc Éla, *My Faith as an African*, p. 19; and Mercy Oduyoye, *Hearing and Knowing*, pp. 73–75.

48. See John S. Pobee, *Toward an African Theology* (Nashville: Abingdon, 1979); John S. Mbiti, *New Testament Eschatology in an African Background* (New York: Oxford University Press, 1971); and Kwesi Dickson and Paul Ellingworth, eds., *Biblical Revelation and African Beliefs* (Maryknoll, N.Y.: Orbis Books, 1969).

49. Pobee writes in *Toward An African Theology*: "Thus the biblical faith allows the possiblity that the natural man, otherwise described as the 'heathen' like our traditional African, has some intimation of God through Creation. Surely all the worship of the traditional African is groping after this divine power, however misguided it may be in parts. Religions, including traditional African religions, would not exist had God not revealed himself, although it is also true that in their attempt to name God, they make for themselves idols, because only God can name himself" (p. 73).

50. See Benjamin Ray, *African Religions*, p. 6–7.

51. See Idowu's essay "God" in Kwesi Dickson and Paul Ellingworth, eds., *Biblical Revelation and African Beliefs* (Maryknoll, N.Y.: Orbis Books, 1969), p. 18.

52. John S. Mbiti, "God, Sin and Religion in African Religion," *The A.M.E. Zion Quarterly Review* 99 (January 1989).

53. See Chris Ifeanyi Ejizu, *Ofo: Igbo Ritual Symbol* (Nigeria: Fourth Dimension Publishing, 1986). In the foreword, Professor Kalu writes: "The study of African traditional religion acquired a new lease on life two decades ago as Africans themselves started a massive attempt to re-understand their cultures. Unfortunately, much emphasis was not paid to methodology and some of the early scholars came from Christian theological and educational backgrounds. The net effects were an enumerative, descriptive approach tainted with Christian bias" (xi).

54. See John S. Mbiti, *Concepts of God in Africa* (London: SPCK, 1979).

55. Michael Kirwen, *The Missionary and the Diviner*, p. 5.

56. Ibid., p. 16.

57. Uli Beir, *Yoruba Myths* (New York: Cambridge University Press, 1980), p. 10.

58. For a fascinating exploration of the Christian meaning of traditional Fon religion, and the Fon meaning of Christianity, see Barthélemy Adoukonou, *Jalons*

pour une théologie africaine. Essai d'une herméneutique chrétienne du Vodun daho-méen. See n. 17 above.

59. See Melville and Frances Herskovits, *An Outline of Dahomean Religious Belief* (Milwood, New York: Kraus Reprint Co., 1976), p. 14. See also Dominique Zahan, *The Religion, Spirituality, and Thought of Traditional Africa*, 11.

60. Anita Glaze, *Art and Death in a Senufo Village* (Bloomington: Indiana University Press, 1981), p. 53.

61. See Rosemary Reuther, *Sexism and God-Talk: Toward a Feminist Theology* (Boston: Beacon Press, 1983), pp. 60–61.

62. John S. Mbiti, "God, Sin, and Salvation in African Religion," *The A.M.E. Zion Quarterly Review* 99 (January 1989): 5.

63. J. Omosade Awolalu, "Sin and Its Removal in African Traditional Religion," *Journal of the American Academy of Religion* 44 (June 1976): 279.

64. Mbiti, "God, Sin, and Salvation," p. 5.

65. Ibid., p. 6.

66. Ibid., p. 7.

67. Michael Kirwen, *The Missionary and the Diviner*, p. 128.

68. Éla discusses the memory of these ancestors, who lost their lives, for example, in Guinea-Bissau, Angola and Mozambique. See *L'Afrique des villages*, p. 226. He explains that African countries that have not gone the disingenuous route of devolution have attained "liberation" through the life-threatening sacrifices of the peasants. Most of these peasants have refused to be divested of their ancestral values. According to Éla, freedom-loving Africans must not forget the contributions of such peasants to the liberation of Africa (p. 227).

69. Amilcar Cabral, *Return to the Source*, p. 54.

70. Jean-Marc Éla, *L'Afrique des villages*, p. 226.

7

Eastern Religions and Liberation

Reflections on an Encounter

JON SOBRINO

It is important to say that many of the issues discussed in this essay are new to me. My remarks were occasioned by my first visit to India. This has given me the chance to listen directly to its religious, theological, and social questions, and I have been very impressed by how new and different this continent is from my experience in Latin America.*

A visit to Asia leads me to express these differences as "tensions"

• anthropologically, between the individual and the community;

• religiously, between the ultimate imaged as holistic-totality and as God;

• within liberation, between *knowledge* of the truth and the *praxis* of love, as means and end of liberation;

• between gnostic and agapaic religions;

• between spirituality and praxis.

Articulating these tensions has been very fruitful for me. It has also made me realize the diverse forms our religious and, more generally, our human nature can assume. Finally, it has made me think about what is positively the most characteristic Christian contribution to human liberation, but also about what are negatively the limitations of Christianity.

Faced with such an accumulation of new ideas and basic problems, the easiest and most honorable response would be to be quiet and reflect for a long time. Since I have been asked, I shall share my thoughts, but I must

---

*Editor's note. This essay is a revised version of an article by the same title, which appeared in *Horizons* 18/1 (1991): 78-92. It is used with the permission of *Horizons*. Translation by Irene B. Hodgson.

also say in advance that what follows are partial and provisional reflections. Furthermore, my reflections are made from the perspectives of Latin American and more particularly Salvadoran Christianity. Such a perspective is both a foundational and a limiting factor in what I have to say.

IN ALL RELIGIONS THERE IS A SEED OF LIBERATION

First, I believe that in every religion there is an important seed of liberation. To understand this claim, we must give concrete meaning to the term "liberation." By liberation I understand that which frees the poor from the proximity of death and encourages them to live. And by the poor we mean those who are oppressed socioeconomically, who are, as a result, near death, and very likely to suffer a violent death when they attempt to work for their liberation. We choose this definition of liberation and correlatively of oppression, because it is the one on which the majority of the people of the Third World would agree. They know full well that their situation is getting worse in a variety of ways, including socioeconomically, and often simply because of race, culture, sex, or caste.

From a religious perspective, as we shall see, liberation is more than freedom from socioeconomic oppression; but we cannot call a religion liberating, in today's world, unless, in some way, it fosters this kind of liberation.

A WAY TO MANAGE LIFE

Before discussing religions and their potential for liberation, I would like to focus on something important that religions, as they exist today in the Third World, can foster. I think that for the poor of this world, religion exercises the primary function of offering a way to *manage life*. That is, faced with the inherent difficulty of surviving and of having a life with some meaning, religion provides a framework in which to live and organize one's life; it proposes a way in which to move forward; it offers meaning and hope; and it gives a measure of dignity.

Such a statement, it is true, comes dangerously close to the idea of religion as an "opiate of the people." Nevertheless, from the perspective we are now taking (which is not yet the perspective of the formally liberating potential of religions), a religion that helps us manage life is not simply an opiate. For we are now talking about life as it has to be lived in the present, not only about future life in a blissful reward. We speak about life that not only has to be endured with resignation (although sometimes that is all one can do), but also as it has to be managed. "To manage life" means simply to live and live with some minimum of meaning, so that life for the poor might not be total chaos. Such a life is a way to live with poverty, with illness, with abandonment, with some minimum of dignity even when faced with indignity. Most of the poor hold on to religion, because often they have nothing else to hold on to. None of the other human institutions that shape history offers them such a handhold. As a general rule, neither governments nor political parties, nor armies, nor the administration of justice, nor economic planning are administered by and for them, and thus the poor find almost nothing in these institutions to hold on to.

Sometimes, it is true, the poor find something in liberation and revolutionary movements, but these too, as necessary and just as they may be, have their limitations today for the majority. In general such movements, however, do not speak to the multitudes, but to groups which, although they may be numerous, do not represent (nor should we expect them to do so) the poor majority as a whole. Even within and during the process of revolution, very concrete needs arise for which the mysticism of revolution does not provide adequate answers for the majority, even though such a revolutionary mysticism may speak powerfully to particular groups.

Whatever we may say about the essence of religion, in the present historical situation religions are carrying out the role of helping the poor "manage life." Often, religion is the only means left by which the poor can manage their lives. For the same reason, though, religions are also historically very *ambiguous*. Oppressors manipulate them precisely because they continue to be so basic for the poor. An example of such manipulation might be found in the proliferation of religious sects in Central America (which is not a topic of simplistic analysis). Their existence is due, in part, to the fact that they respond to a series of religious and human needs to which no one else seems to give a better response. For their members, they can be "the only thing that helps them." In addition, and no less importantly, the manipulation of religious traditions by those in power is also evident.

We are saying, therefore, that in the present world, filled with massive injustice and with little prospect for change, religion is normally the only thing left for the poor to hold on to, to manage their lives. From this, I conclude, on the one hand, that religions have value and, on the other hand, that they must not be romanticized, because at the present time there is also an active attempt to manipulate them.

IS THEIR CAPACITY FOR LIBERATION REAL?

In addition to the ability to "manage life" offered by religions, we must also examine their formally liberating capacity. This capacity can be considered, I suggest, from two questions: (1) What is there in the core of a specific religion, as it normally appears in its sacred writings, that is liberating? (2) Is that specific liberating message historicized in the present and, if so, how? It seems to me important to analyze both issues. The first question helps to clarify what, in a specific religion, is meant by liberation. The second offers criteria for historical verification that will help prevent the discourse about the liberating capacity of religions from being simply voluntaristic, or abstract, and, therefore, ineffective.

By reason of their sacred writings and history, the Abrahamic religions can claim an essential liberating capacity. This is certainly clear in Christianity and Judaism, at least in its Old Testament form, but also in Islam, as modern Muslim exegesis attests. The liberation of the poor is central to these religions in at least four ways: (1) at the *cognitive level*, in their central message and afterwards in their doctrines; (2) at the *ethical level*, insofar as a religion affirms liberation as a necessary good that must be put into practice, in opposition to oppression; (3) at the *level of praxis* in the dialectic of liberation as a gift given by God but carried out by human beings; and (4) at the *eschatological level*, where liberation is used to describe ultimate and definitive reality.

What of traditions other than the Abrahamic? In India, I heard an exegesis of certain sacred Scriptures of Asian religions in which social criticism and the ideal means for social transformation, that is, liberation, are central. Without wishing to overgeneralize, I believe that liberation is central to the sacred writings of religions, although in different forms and degrees, and is something that we must affirm and emphasize nowadays. It identifies religion (to the extent that it is liberating) as a historically available reality to which the poor can turn for their self-understanding, their hope, their struggle, and their liberation. The concerns of the poor are expressed in religion, which indicates that the desire for life is the motivating factor in religion, that the correlation between God and life is primary, and that, therefore, the poor believe connaturally in the God of life. Religion contains the basic ethical affirmation that giving life is good, and that good is fundamentally defined as giving life.

These ideas are not new. They are, for instance, a product of what I see happening in Latin America. For example, I find it very revealing that in Latin America, "liberation" has been associated linguistically with religions through "liberation theology." This does not mean that liberation has not been related to other dimensions of life and history. There exist, certainly, political and revolutionary movements that understand themselves as liberating. There is also a "pedagogy of liberation." But, at least in present-day usage, expressions such as "liberation medicine," "liberation law," "liberation engineering," and so forth, have not taken hold. Of course, phenomena should not be analyzed only in terms of the name given them. But it is still worth noting that the term "liberation" has been associated in Latin America fundamentally with religious reality. This indicates, at least, that liberation exists at the heart of this way of being religious. Perhaps, in the real life of most people, liberation — as ideal, as hope, and as demand — is better expressed and is more active in religion than in many other areas of life.

AGAPAIC AND GNOSTIC RELIGIONS

To these reflections, I wish to add others that have occurred to me as I have become better acquainted with Asian religions. I am only going to mention those things that have given me most to think about insofar as they are different from and challenging to Christianity. I am not going to dwell on the challenge to Christianity, which seems very clear to me, but rather offer some reflections, or "reactions," on how it is possible to integrate, from a Christian point of view, what the Asian religions, especially in India, are and demand. In doing this, I will touch on points that, directly or indirectly, concern liberation.

Religions have sometimes been classified, usually by Christians, as "gnostic" and "agapaic." And although both elements are acknowledged by such scholars as somehow present in all religions, gnosis is usually considered the predominant element in Asian religions and agape in the Abrahamic ones. For our purposes, it is important to note that, at least in theory, both elements are considered liberating. From a Christian perspective, the question is how to give value to the element of gnosis within agape.

Historically, we can find parallels in gnostic Christianity, for example, in the second century and later. We could also look into the phenomenon of mysticism. To my way of understanding, however, we are better advised to explore whether and how Christianity can foster gnosis from that which is, theoretically, more specifically characteristic of Christianity—in other words, from agape.

Of course, Christianity simultaneously affirms the will to know truth and to make truth a historical reality. It says that the one who does not love does not see and the one who does love sees—God. As we have said elsewhere, "The one who goes toward God sees God." From this perspective, at least, there is no negation of gnosis, although it is true that it is still subordinated in some way to agape. What must be stressed is the capacity of agape itself to reveal the truth. I think that the one who truly loves knows, so that, negatively, if love does not produce knowledge, that is to say, *if it does not produce gnosis*, one could doubt that it is true love.

Perhaps one can argue that in this vision, the dimension of the gratuitous self-manifestation of truth is not so obvious. In a Christian sense, however, I think that the grace is, or should be, as clear in loving as in knowing. When agape is not purely human hubris, nor exaggerated Pelagianism, when love is made possible by the prior great love of God, then grace is present in agape. And my intuition is that when agape is gratuitous, then it will foster gnosis and this gnosis will liberate.

Put in a negative form, the well-known text of Romans 1:18ff. supposes the possibility of the knowledge of truth, but it also stresses that its greatest difficulty consists not in limitation (in not finding the right path or proper techniques), but in a primordial act of the spirit: *oppressing truth with injustice.* This oppression is mainly a matter of ethical praxis, and, therefore, to reach true gnosis, it is necessary (1) to overcome oppression, and (2) to liberate the spirit from its innate oppressive tendency.

I seek to emphasize the importance that the element of gnosis has in religions and my conviction that true liberation, as much for its wholeness as for its historical efficacy, should integrate gnosis and agape. What I have tried to add is that in Christianity, as well as in Asian religions, gnosis ought to be present through agape, which would be in its specific presupposition.

"CREATION" AS SACRAMENT AND AS "INSTRUMENT"

The observation that, for Asian religions, creation is seen as a sacrament, while for Western religions (and certainly for the Western world), creation is seen more as an instrument, seems to me important. A crucial implication of this, with respect to liberation, is that a purely instrumental vision of creation dehumanizes instead of liberates. It does so by oppressing the humanness of humankind, while the sacramental vision liberates.

I think that Christianity also gives a serious warning against sheer instrumentalization of creation. The previously mentioned passage from Romans 1:18ff. states that by oppressing the truth of things we deprive them of their ability to reveal God; that is, they are desacramentalized. At the same time, the heart is darkened and becomes the prey of perdition; that is, it is dehumanized.

What I would like to add is that, from the perspective of Christianity (not of the practice of the Western world), this negative, instrumentalized vision of creation can be overcome in another way. It seems to me that the instrumentalized vision, which is very real, destructive, and dehumanizing, is pernicious, precisely because it looks upon the things of creation as an extension of the individual and, thus, may even consider them solely for the benefit of the individual. Such an attitude implies an egoistical appropriation of creation. In reality, the concrete realities of creation can and should serve as mediators for right relations among human beings, as mediators of justice, of love, and ultimately of the Kingdom of God. Creation realities, therefore, are humanized when they foster not the dominance of the individual human being over them, and through them over other human beings, but rather when they promote solidarity. Also, I think this vision of creation as mediator of fellowship can facilitate the sacramental vision. This enables natural objects to speak for themselves and to find expression in culture and art. I do not believe we can draw a fully developed answer to the contemporary problem from St. Francis of Assisi, but at least we can point out his dual passion for creation and solidarity. So, from a Christian perspective, created realities can be seen as mediators of solidarity. They are to be respected in their natural state and are, in the final analysis, sacraments of God. Of course, historically, there is very little of the Franciscan spirit in a Western world that oppresses and ravages both nature and human beings.

THE EXPERIENCE OF LOSING AND FINDING ONESELF IN THE WHOLE

A third thing I wish to comment on is the "holistic" experience that the Asian religions foster, as fruit of gnosis. This is an experience that is not only declared in doctrine, but is realized by concrete individuals, some of them Christians. If I have understood correctly, it is an experience of wholeness, of becoming one with (or losing and finding oneself in) everything, of resonating totally with reality, eliminating the division between subject and object. Within this experience, I have sensed what might be called a totalizing and reconciling spirit that is part of the metaphysical mentality underlying Asian religions and cultures. I would like to comment on what this experience brings to liberation, on what challenge it offers the Christian tradition, and on what Asian religions might find in Christianity.

In light of what I hear said about such experiences and orientations, I believe them to be enriching and liberating. Furthermore, I think that, in principle, the desire to be reconciled with the whole is part of human nature. As has been recognized, here the Eastern religions may have a clear advantage over other religions.

In what follows, I will not be able to explore my surprise that, in the wholeness envisioned by Asian religions, divinity need not be all-inclusive, for it can also be an element included, along with others, within totality. Rather, I would like to raise some questions that have occurred to me and consider some answers that Christianity can offer to these questions.

The first question is about the personal-individual dimension of the Asian experience, that is, about the extent to which, at least in theory, it can do without the communitarian dimension. The second question is about the spiritual dimensions that, again in theory, might exist without praxis. I am not saying that either the communitarian or the praxis elements are negated, but I am suggesting that, although for other reasons they may be worthy of praise and should be fostered, it has not been proven that both elements are essential to holistic experience.

These are the questions that, from the perspective of Christianity, the holistic experience suggests to me. But questions must also be asked the other way around: Is there anything of this holistic experience within Christianity? What can and should be learned from Eastern religions? Leaving aside mystic experiences within Christianity, it seems to me that Christianity contains a quality that, at first sight, makes the holistic or undifferentiated part of the mystical experience of total unity difficult to accept. On an ethical level—though not on the metaphysical level—there is a strong dualism or dialectic tension in Christianity (for example, between grace and sin; between life and death; between God and evil) that does not favor a holistic or monistic spirit, but rather a passionate taking of sides, of making choices. It is said, also, that in Christianity there are concrete and privileged contexts for the experience of God or for spiritual experience in general (according to liberation theology, this context is the poor of this world). Christians stress that the human being realizes him- or herself through the practice of love, of mercy, following the examples of Moses, the Good Samaritan, and, of course, Jesus.

As a thesis, we can say that in Christianity, the human being is realized not only through liberating the self, but also by making a choice in favor of something and against—not only doing without—something else, that is, by the praxis of loving the oppressed and acting against those who have created oppression.

Does this mean that because of the nature of Christian praxis and the choice between mutually exclusive alternatives, the experience of an undifferentiated whole is impossible or difficult within Christianity? I believe that holistic experience does occur among Christians and would explain it by noting that the Christian vision is holistic to the extent that it believes that it is possible to "gain everything," that is, life. Negatively, in order to gain, one has to be prepared to "lose everything." Positively, one has to live for others. But this necessary existence-for-others has coexistence as a limit (although nowadays this term has been devalued). Living for others implies the hope of being able to achieve being-with-others. Historically, both moments are related only dialectically; thus the praxis of living-for-others is already integrated (although provisionally, sometimes fleetingly) in being-with-others. This constitutes the holistic part of Christian experience. Christianity says that there will be true holistic experience only at the end, when God will be all in all, and when charity (the only thing that lasts forever) no longer has the form of being-for but that of being-with.

But the always provisional quality of the holistic experience does not change the fact that it can happen in history "now," at any time. Expressed in more theological language, the life of human beings, as they follow Jesus, includes the abasement of becoming flesh in the most painful aspects of reality. This enfleshment requires one to announce and practice the Good News and to bear the sin of the world that reacts against this news and leads to the cross. All this can be lived with the values of the resurrection— hope, liberty, and joy. In systematic language, perhaps we can say that the specifically Christian form of having holistic experience in history is to live a resurrected life within history.

What I have expressed so far in abstract form has a very real counterpart. From what I have seen in others and felt in myself, a Mass for the martyrs in El Salvador, for example, can become a holistic experience. At such a liturgy, a series of elements come together in unity, elements which, when unified, allow us to live in wholeness, even if only for a moment. Later reflection differentiates them as elements of love and hope, of sin and grace, of faith and history, of church and people, of human action and the presence of God, of the earth whose fruits are offered and of evocative music, and of hard demands to continue the work of fallen martyrs. This grows out of knowing oneself to have a responsibility that cannot be delegated, and of knowing oneself with others and carried by others. It is a holistic experience of both fear and joy, of immediate present and fullness of future. Whatever form this phenomenon takes, I want to emphasize that in these moments, what speaks to us is the totality of reality. One is immersed in this totality. It reminds me a little of the disappearance of the separation of subject-object.

In the light of the above, I say that the holistic experience is important, and that it is also important for religions to foster it. Such experience is both important and liberating. On the whole, I think that Eastern religions try more explicitly to foster such experiences, while Christianity tends to be purely doctrinal (at its worst) or purely ethical-practical (in many of its reform movements). But I think also that Christianity, as I have tried to explain, offers the possibility of holistic experience, although such experience is more related to the liberation of the poor. In my opinion, it is from this experience (spoken of by Gustavo Gutiérrez or Pedro Casaldáliga, though in different ways) that the commitment to liberation draws its life. Such holistic experience is the guarantee that the commitment to liberation endures over the long run, and that it is liberating also for those who practice it.

A LIBERATING RELIGION MUST LIBERATE

With the previous reflections, I have tried to analyze and revalue what it is that is liberating in religions, and how it might be experienced. Now I would like to add that for real liberation to take place in the present, the return to founding origins and to sacred writings is important, necessary, and useful, but it is not sufficient.

To realize liberation in the present, it is very useful and normally necessary to analyze the founding sacred Scriptures in order to determine what in their message is truly liberating. In Latin America, it is evident that the decision for and practice of liberation have been greatly fostered by the reading of the Old and New Testaments (though this is usually a rereading, meant to be more faithful to the text) and the determination of the fundamental truth of the Bible. The same can be said of the rereading of the history of the church, especially of the church in Latin America in its origins in the sixteenth century.

By determining the truth about origins, one can remove antiliberating attitudes and both deideologize and unmask viewpoints based on incorrect interpretations of the original writings. Such a liberating rereading of the Scriptures is helpful in encouraging the practice of liberation and in offering direction for this practice, even though such directions may be quite generic and utopian. The practice encouraged by the Scriptures usually places the necessary sociohistorical liberation within a more inclusive globalizing and even transcendent ideal of liberation.

But, this said, it is necessary to stress that a religion has a capacity for liberation only if it shows it in the present. Tautology though this be, it is important to remember it so that we do not repeat and even glory in a liberating capacity of religions that we cannot verify. For a religion to be considered liberating, we must be able to analyze and verify two things.

The first is the capacity of the "essence" of a religion to historicize its origin in the present. In biblical language, this is the ability to discover the "signs of the times," the ability to actualize the presence and will of the divine. Theologically, that means to concentrate not only on the study of origins, but also on theological analysis of the present in light of the religion's self-understanding. Expressed in hypothetical terms, if a religion is not compelled, by its own nature, to focus on the present, or if, upon focusing on the present, it finds a complete lack of continuity with its origin, that religion would be ineffective today as far as liberation is concerned. As I understand it, that is not what is happening today, and the religions that want to be liberating do find continuity between the praxis of liberation and their historical origins. But what I want to stress is that it is not enough to remember the liberating roots of a religion, as happens, for example, in good exegesis of the Old and New Testaments in the First World, unless, in reality, the Christian religion commits itself to liberation.

The second point is to analyze the contribution of formal religion to liberation. In the historic process of liberation, many elements are present, many of which do not come from religion, but from other sources. For example, unbearable situations may lead to conscientization. Marxism may also become a source of conscientization. Religion, therefore, has a double task. In the first place, it must insert itself into historical liberation movements, because there are important points at which these and religion coincide.

In the second place, religion must not simply fit into other movements. Rather, it must make a formally religious contribution to liberation by enabling faith to contribute to liberation through elements that are specifically religious. This is what is happening, I would say, in many places in Latin America. Faith is motivating believers not only to participate in liberating tasks and movements, but also to contribute a positive and critical ingredient to the process of liberation. Thus, positively, liberation is enabled to actualize itself more deeply and to be filled with increasingly human values and with a more specifically Christian spirit (clearer vision, mercy, hope against hope, and so forth). Negatively, the religious ingredient helps cure the undesirable by-products that are generated in the liberation process, such as dogmatism, divisiveness, and a tendency to mysticize violence.

To analyze whether a religion is liberating, we must analyze it in the present, in its various social settings, to see whether *in fact* it encourages rather than hinders specific liberation movements, whether it is able to be integrated in them, and whether it is able to contribute to these movements a religious content that will empower and protect them.

CONFLICT AS INHERENT IN ANY LIBERATING RELIGION

What I have said up to now is what I was led to reflect on most during my encounters in Asia. Now I would like to add two reflections. The first concerns religions and conflict. The second revolves around ecumenism.

Perhaps because of the situation in which I have lived for many years, and because of my understanding of Christianity, I have noticed that in our discussions, conflict has not been mentioned when talking about the topic of religions and liberation. It seems to me that religions are generally based on the ideal of unity and reconciliation among all things. This is clearly the case for those religions that have Divine Being as the source of ultimate and founding unity. But even for those religions that affirm an all-encompassing Absolute, there is the intuition that multiplicity does not guarantee meaning, and that diversity is always a penultimate stage. The longing for final reconciliation and unity are characteristic of the Abrahamic religions. Eastern holistic experience, such as I understand it, indicates the possibility of directly experiencing the goodness of unity and reconciliation already existing now in history.

I think that most religions would formally agree that this ideal of unity and reconciliation, however, is not a mere empirical datum. Quite the contrary, it is something that has to be realized. And here is where conflict enters. From a Christian perspective, conflict is not only something recognized as an undeniable historical fact, but also something into which the religious human being, of necessity, has to be introduced, insofar as he or she is human and religious. The ideal of unity and reconciliation cannot be achieved by avoiding conflict, but only by taking on conflict. At a personal level, this is well described by the term "conversion," which presupposes not only going outside oneself toward God, but also acting against oneself. And such conversion-as-conflict, I wish to suggest, also occurs on the historical, social, and structural levels.

From the perspective of Christianity, religions that try to be liberating will discover that the world that they want to liberate is not only limited, but also sinful. That is, not only has the world not yet become what it ought to be, but also, to a great extent, it is the opposite of what it ought to be. The reality of the world *is* diametrically opposed to what it *should be* and works against those who want to transform it into what it should be.

Expressed in biblical language, not only does the Kingdom of God not exist in its fullness, but attempts to make it grow do not start on a level playing field. Instead, our efforts are carried out from within an anti-Kingdom world that resists attempts to instill the values of God. If we use the term "mediation" for the carrying out of the divine will, and if we call the person or groups that carry it out "mediators," we have to affirm that the relationship between the mediation of the true God (the Kingdom of God) and the mediations of other false divinities (all kinds of historical-social oppressive configurations) is conflictive and antagonistic. We see this clearly in the history of concrete mediators. Those who foster true mediation (the Kingdom of God) necessarily enter into conflict with the mediators of other divinities. Is that not what we learn from the lives of such persons as Mahatma Gandhi, Archbishop Romero, and Martin Luther King? In Christian language, this dialectic is concretized as a struggle between the God of life and the divinities of death (historical realities that function as true idols which demand worship and victims to continue to exist).

All of this shows that conflict is something connatural to religious experience, because sin exists in history and shapes the world in a form not only different from but contrary to the will of God. If this is so, we see the obvious paradox that the true God and God's mediators seem to lose in the struggle. That sin has power is the great aporia of history, which can bring about that religion, as religion, proposes resignation as the only appropriate way to manage life. In a similar vein, religions can propose an other-worldly hope as the only way finally to resolve the paradox of history. In both proposals, conflict is avoided.

But for Christianity, it is essential to maintain absolutely unshakable its mandate to announce and initiate the Kingdom of God in this world in the presence of and in opposition to the anti-Kingdom. Conflict is, then, inevitable. It is characteristic of Christianity to hope (many times against hope) that progress is possible in the historical realization of the Kingdom of God in this world, and to demand insistently a form of praxis to make this Kingdom real.

Therefore, as is clearly the case in Latin America, the different Christian confessions, by being what they are, have found themselves in sharp conflict with the powers of this world. This is the fundamental conflict they face. At a secondary level, there are conflicts inside the churches, but not fundamentally for reasons of orthodoxy and discipline, but rather because of their taking a position in opposition to the world.

I want to close these reflections about conflict with a note of caution. In affirming that religion must take on conflict, we must be careful to place conflict in the correct perspective and not make it into something mystical. It can, and often does, happen that, in the name of religion, conflict and struggle become fanaticized, and the necessity of dying and killing is introduced. It is well known that religion can be a mechanism for generating fanaticism. So when we talk about conflict, we are neither encouraging suicide nor exalting suffering and death.

But, with this caution, we cannot deny the conflictive nature of religion. When religion becomes a generator of liberation, it automatically provokes conflict. By their historical nature, some religions will have more of a tendency to do this than others. But it is impossible to avoid all conflict. In provoking conflict, religion imbues it with other values—mercy, dialogue, forgiveness, a reversal of fanaticism, a mysticism of peace. On the other hand, it also offers firmness and strength and is aware of the possibility of martyrdom, recognizing that the martyr is victim both of sin (and thus an indictment of the instruments of death) and of holiness (and thus an example of the greater love that leads one to give one's life for others).

AN ECUMENISM OF RELIGIONS TO SAVE HUMANITY

Today we often hear that religious ecumenism is very important for the peace of the world. Insofar as the majority of humanity is still religious, this means, at the least, that ecumenism can serve to minimize conflicts of a religious character. In a positive sense, it also presupposes that in religion in any of its forms, there is something good and positive that can unite human beings to work for peace and promote greater social justice and commitment to such things as liberation.

Personally, I share this view, even though history also shows that religious ecumenism is not at all easy, and that one often encounters cases where religious commitments contribute to the conflicts, injustices, and struggles among different religions. I believe that the various religions should enrich, dialogue with, and complement one another, without thinking that any one of them (even those that believe themselves to be the true religions) have a historical monopoly on all human and transcendent religious values.

The consideration I would like to add deals with the minimal level on which the different religions can and, in my opinion, should unite to make religious ecumenism something good for the world and fruitful for each one of the religions.

According to the formal schema I referred to before, reality can be discovered theologically according to the following categories: (1) divinity; (2) mediators of divinity (persons or groups); and (3) mediations of divinity (historical configuration of human social reality). For religious ecumenism (and even for final salvation according to the Christian faith), we must begin with mediation. On what minimal configuration of historical reality might the different religious traditions agree and even complement and enrich each other without betraying their own principles?

To formulate the mediation we can use terminologies such as those I have heard proposed—for example, Kingdom of God in Abrahamic formulations, and absolute future or absolute present in Hindu formulations. The different formulations already indicate different understandings of what we have called mediation. But, regardless of the differences between terminologies, a minimal formulation, I maintain, should include (1) overcoming of socioeconomic, racial, cultural, and sexual oppression; (2) enhancing social life in structures furthering justice in human relations, dignity through recognition of the value of human beings, peace through struggling against the causes of war, and by justly resolving conflicts; and (3) fostering spiritual values among human beings via their cultures, their art, their religious traditions and so forth.

This is a description of a possible Utopia. By calling it "minimal," I refer not to its realization in history, which would be a great "maximum," but, with a view to ecumenism, to that minimum necessary for religions to formulate shared visions of a "common" Utopia. We need such positive shared visions, in contrast to the utopias of the powerful of this world—empires and conquests over others at the scientific, technological, and economic levels.

To agree on a "minimal" level of mediation is, ultimately, to understand ecumenism in relation to the poor of the world. Undoubtedly, the way in which "mediator" and "divinity" are understood will influence the understanding of "mediation." Still, it seems to me both easier and more urgent to begin ecumenism by agreeing on the construction of a more just, fraternal, and human world.

To express what I mean in the form of an anecdote, and a negative one at that, I remember being told in England that ecumenism between Anglicans and Roman Catholics was progressing. But, my informant added, that did not seem at all good to him, since those who—at the level of mediation—were most backward were the ones agreeing on the terms of the emerging common understandings. Such ecumenism will not benefit but worsen the situation of the poor.

On a positive note, I favor the movement towards forming "human base communities." This presupposes the possibility of joining together on the basis of our humanness and of those aspects of our humanity that more or less lead to the kind of mediation that I have described above. In this way of proceeding, members of various religions and ideologies (as well as members of diverse "denominations" within these groups) who agree on the need to change this world of injustice and to foster human values band together.

In conclusion, I realize that what I have said is only a "reaction," mainly from the perspective of Christian faith and of El Salvador. I do not wish even to appear to claim expertise on the world of Asian religions, either in its attractive features or in its limitations. Nevertheless, from a strictly religious point of view, I believe that Christianity must open itself to the Asian spirit, even if only to moderate its own intolerance with the Asian spirit of tolerance. On the other hand, the Asian world can perhaps be enriched by the spirit of the Christian ethos and praxis, so that its "tolerance" does not become indifference. From a historical point of view, it is imperative that Christianity not be considered only a manifestation of the "West" with its baggage of political, cultural, and religious oppression. Rather, one can hope that the people of Asia will be able to distinguish what is Western in Christianity from what is human, Abrahamic in the broadest sense and "Jesuanic" in the strict sense. Perhaps what is happening in Latin America can help us to make this distinction clear, although, in comparison with Asia, even the present-day liberating Christianity of Latin America can seem to be too Western.

At any rate, for me, the most important result of the encounter with the religions of Asia has been to become conscious again that the situation of the Third World demands an urgent solution. This is why we must bring about a better mutual understanding and unification of diverse religious traditions, so that each of them can contribute as best it can to the task of liberation.

8

Commensurability and Ambiguity

Liberation as an Interreligiously Usable Concept

WILLIAM R. BURROWS

Jon Sobrino makes two observations in his reflections on Eastern religions and liberation. These observations, which structure this chapter are: (1) that in every religion there is a "seed of liberation," even though sometimes its contribution to human liberation may extend only to helping the poor manage life in the face of oppressive power; but also (2) that religions are often manipulated by those in power. Each of the contributors to *World Religions and Human Liberation* in one way or another makes the first point. The agenda for future discussion pointed to by all these chapters, however, lurks behind the problems contained in two words: *commensurability* and *ambiguity*. To Sobrino's observation that religion can function ambiguously because of its potentiality for manipulation by the powerful (an extrinsic ambiguity), I add Tillich's note that in and of itself religion is intrinsically ambiguous, sometimes radically so:

Religion as the self-transcending function of life, claims to be the answer to the ambiguities of life in all other dimensions; it transcends their finite tensions and conflicts. But in doing so, it falls into even profounder tensions, conflicts and ambiguities. Religion is the highest expression of the greatness and dignity of life; in it the greatness of life becomes holiness. Yet religion is also the most radical refutation of the greatness and dignity of life; in it the great becomes most profanized, the holy most desecrated. These ambiguities are the central subject of any honest dealing with religion, and they are the background with which church and theology must work.[1]

COMMENSURABILITY

By the term commensurability, I mean the problem of multiple meanings of words, such as "liberation," in the world's religious traditions. Although the discussion of commensurability as a problem in cross-cultural communication can be highly technical, I use it here in a relatively straightforward, ordinary-language fashion. For our purposes, to be commensurable a word, a concept, or a linked family of words and concepts in one historical-linguistic tradition (for example, "liberation" in Western Christian theology) must denote, connote, or meaningfully "measure" a similarly linked family of words and concepts in another tradition (for example, in Zen Buddhism). If it does, comparisons and contrasts between these traditions can be made with some degree of clarity. If not, apples may be unfairly measured against oranges, mules against tractors, or the Christian goal of liberation against the Indian religious goal of *nirvana* or *moksha*.

The question: Is the word "liberation" used in a *sufficiently analogous manner* by another religious tradition that it can be properly considered a valid indicator of that tradition's orientation toward human vocation and thus be compared with what liberation theologians maintain is or ought to be central to the Christian tradition? Extending the question further: Is liberation, as understood by liberation theology, a candidate for articulating socio-cultural-political-economic emancipation as a universal human value? It has been suggested by Paul Knitter, for example, that a liberationist "soteriocentrism" is possibly this sort of notion.[2]

First, it is necessary to say very emphatically that Westerners need to take to heart Joseph Kitagawa's observation that Asian social reform movements "do not imply the universalization of Western concepts, as it is often interpreted in some Western circles." Rather, as Kitagawa goes on to say, while not rejecting Western influence, "Easterners ... are appropriating certain features of Western civilization *to enrich their own world of meanings.*"[3]

It is helpful to recall the dynamics that led to the emergence of liberation theology in Western Christian tradition. In this regard, we should first note that "liberation" derives from a constellation of words revolving around "salvation." They were used originally to characterize the result of events such as the exodus of Israel from Egypt and the resurrection of Jesus from the dead. In time, from these narratives were derived symbols and doctrines engendering hope for a final eschatological liberation of the cosmos from the powers of sin and death. In that escatological act, God, it is believed, perhaps more importantly "hoped," will act to liberate creation, including humanity, from bondage. Liberation theology accentuates the human side of the salvation-as-liberation equation, but insofar as it is organically Christian, the discussion and the activity take place in relationship to final salvation imaged as a gift of God accomplished in and through Yeshua of

Nazareth, whom the New Testament calls the Messiah or the Christ.

Second, one must note that with the dawn of the modern era, the plausibility of ancient and medieval syntheses on salvation and the relation of time and eternity began collapsing among intellectual elites. But this synthesis was also the regnant interpretation of the classic biblical narratives (that is, on the Exodus, Resurrection, and Pentecost—as a symbol of the church's birth as a pneumatic, not simply a christologic event). When all this collapsed for Western elites, Christian identity was thrown into doubt. The result was that "modernizers" began to experience talk about eternal salvation as alienating believers from their responsibilities to improve the temporal world. Eternal salvation-talk, accordingly, became embarrassing to many moderns, and the Christian "eschatology office" (Ernst Troeltsch's ironic remark) nearly went out of business.[4]

In a major interpretive moment, figures such as Schleiermacher in the Protestant tradition and Loisy (two generations later) in the Catholic dealt with the collapse of the medieval world view by attempting to show the compatibility of Christian faith and modern culture. Although there were profound differences between them, a family of linked responses coalesced around reinterpreting Jewish and Christian traditions in response to the modern *Zeitgeist.* That was, of course, the beginning of "liberal" theology, which flourished in Protestantism and Judaism. It was stifled in Catholicism, and in the aftermath of the horrors of the Holocaust, liberal Judaism's assimilationist directions have been seriously questioned. Liberation theology, however, represents a more radical proposal for reinterpreting Christian identity and vocation than does liberal theology. Deane William Ferm, in his summary of the tenets of liberation theology, has indicated the main lines of this movement. He does so, however, without rooting liberation theology in classical christology, which could give the impression that all Latin Americans evacuate christology of its "orthodox" soteriological content. Dan Cohn-Sherbok gives a much more nuanced and correct account of this dimension. Gustavo Gutiérrez, in a careful summary of the foundations of his theology, for example, takes pains to avoid the tendency of many to ignore the specificity of Christian liberation theology:

> The great hermeneutic principle of faith and, therefore, of all [Christian] theological discourse is Jesus Christ. He is the revealer of the Father; in him all things have been created and redeemed (see Colossians 1:15–20).[5]

For Gutiérrez, classic christology and soteriology receive new emphases, but they are not thereby denied. Gutiérrez is not, in other words, a liberal or postmodern theologian seeking to revise the basic structure of Christian belief, even though he is wary of letting a concentration of "eternal" dimensions of salvation crowd out "temporal" liberation. Moreover, he goes far beyond the liberal nonaggression pact with modernity when he begins with the experience of the poor and oppressed and seeks to amplify their voices in ways that call into serious question the structures of modern life — theologically, socially, politically, culturally, and economically. And all this is part of Gutiérrez's conviction that liberation is an intrinsic aspect of *Christian* evangelization.[6] The acceptance of christological orthodoxy creates major problems in the area of the usefulness of liberation theology for members of other religious traditions. We shall not discuss them at great length here, but it is only honest to admit that to the extent that the "uniqueness" of Christianity is interpreted to make the way of Jesus the "sole" valid way, liberation theology is ambiguous for members of other religious ways.

The question we seek to discuss is whether the sweeping restructuring of the regnant systems of economics and social control advocated by liberation theology finds resonance in the various world religions. Is the term, in other words, commensurable?

We begin with Dan Cohn-Sherbok's "Judaism and Liberation Theology." In effect, Cohn-Sherbok finds no practical wall between the ideals of liberation theology and Judaism, provided one prescinds from specific Christian theological claims of the sort Gutiérrez gives as his theological warrants. Cohn-Sherbok, I have noted, is very careful to delineate where Judaism and Christianity agree and where they part company. He judges, overall, that they are in concert in retrieving the prophetic strand of the Hebrew biblical tradition. In the struggle to effect the Kingdom, according to Cohn-Sherbok, liberation theology and the rabbinic theology become one in their goal.

Most Christians will agree with Jews such as Cohn-Sherbok on the importance of working to improve human conditions and of seeing the human vocation to do this as having a relationship to manifesting or effecting the Reign of God on earth. Whether such Christians also envisage the role of the church as having a leading role in shaping social transformation is another matter. The same question put to Jews about Judaism, I suspect, will yield equally varied results. Nevertheless, in terms of conceptual commensurability, Jews and Christians have a sufficiently analogous vocabulary that they can delineate accurately where they disagree and where they agree. Cohn-Sherbok's chapter is evidence of that.

Muhammad Mashuq ibn Ally's "Theology of Islamic Liberation" reveals a similar dynamic. Although there are clear differences between Ally and Cohn-Sherbok, Sobrino, and Ferm, the analogies are also sufficiently clear that a meaningful conversation can occur in the context of fundamentally similar world views.

Ally powerfully drives home the fact that modernity has marginalized God and that the resultant secularism dehumanizes society by obscuring the divine origin and goal of creation. *Umma*, for Ally, is the goal of Islamic liberation movements: "a New Order which ensures justice for all human beings" and that will "bring them back to their original source — Islam."

For Muslims, the root cause of social evil is alienation from God. Christians and Jews may agree that this is true, but my judgment is that even when they *say* this, most do so with far less specific content in mind than do Muslims for whom the Qur'an is not something to be *interpreted* in the light of modern experience but something to be *implemented*.[7]

In reading Ally, I am reminded of the goals of medieval Christendom: maintaining a social structure that reflects the eternal order established by the Creator.[8] Now for many, the word "medieval" evokes the "Dark Ages." I do not mean anything remotely resembling that simplistic misinterpretation. Rather, I have been led by Ernst Troeltsch to see the medieval cultural-political-religious synthesis as a powerful concretization of the Christian vision of the divine-human relationship.[9] Medieval civilization portrayed unity between time and eternity and provided an anchor for values. But it was also a construal of human existence over against an eternal cosmic structure that is at fundamental odds with the modern West's.

The medieval vision, as distinguished from the modern, was not one of a universal relativity and one whose bondage to oppressive powers was accidental and reversible by human effort. Rather, the bondage was considered a permanent brake on human efforts, and the role of Christians, especially princes and the hierarchy of the church, was to alleviate the effects of disordered life insofar as that was possible under the limitations of original sin. The world and its problems, for classic Western Christianity, were an ever-present challenge to spiritual growth and a challenge to church efforts to wean humans from setting their sights too low. It was exactly this view of the world of spirit as the really real that modernity challenged as alienating Christians from the temporal world.

In the Muslim view, as it is discussed ably by Ally, the Christian medieval cultural-religious-political synthesis is both right and wrong. Right in believing that human-being is understood only when seen in relation to God and submitting to the divine rule. Wrong insofar as contemporary Christianity sets its sights too low, not seeing the realizability of *umma* on earth.

The goal of Islam is to overcome the split between the world as it is and the teaching of Muhammad. On the Muslim reading of religion and culture, the medieval Christian mistake (overaccentuating the eschatological or the transcendent) is minor in comparison with contemporary Christian acquiescence in the split beween "religion and the state." Accepting the autonomy of the secular world and of the individual is a fatally wrong step to take, in the view of Ally, since then "the conquest of nature [becomes] the main target of human effort, and the stream of civilization is allowed to run its course without reference to the values and principles communicated to humanity by God through his prophets." Ally realizes that similar problems plague the world of Islam, but notes that at least there are strong currents there trying to bring Islam back to its senses. In the culture of the post-Christian West, on the contrary, Ally detects a flight from the principle of "natural religion" as embracing all human beings.

In terms of the commensurability question, it is clear that Christians, Jews, and Muslims have enough common ground to debate meaningfully such issues. The encyclicals of John Paul II, for instance, could be proffered by Christians as an example of how a major force within Christianity attempts to bring both old things and new into conversation.

Still, there is an important question for Christians. Is it possible that liberation as vocation to transform the social order is more natural to Muslim and Jewish traditions than to the Christian? Does liberation theology owe the origin of its option for the poor as much to Marxian critiques as to the historical Jesus?

Although I acknowledge the important work done in retrieving the socio-historical dimensions of Jesus and earliest Christianity,[10] the *novum* in Christianity, on balance, lies not in its love ethic or Jesus' resistance to oppression. In all that, Jesus can be seen to be simply a good Jew of a certain sort. Jewish tradition, for example, abounds in teachings as antilegalistic as his. Nor was Jesus especially radical in the attempt to purify the Temple and its priesthood, for reformers with the same program abounded (the Essenes, for example). Nor in linking genuine worship and concern for the neighbor, for that was also at the heart of both Deuteronomic and Pharisaic reform movements.

The *novum* in Christianity, I believe, was the belief that the man who taught and did all this was uniquely the eschatological Son of God, himself the new Temple, whose Spirit would regenerate those who followed him. The earliest strands of the New Testament struggle to articulate that conviction in ways understandable to Jewish and Hellenistic culture.[11] As Christianity moved into the Greco-Roman world, the messages of Easter and Pentecost, with their symbology of eschatologic finality, were thus transmuted into a message of Jesus the Christ, redeemer, consubstantial Son of God offering the gift of eternal life. It was further transmuted into faith in the church as mediator of saving grace and exemplar of the eternal heavenly order as the divine order embodied in the Roman Empire waned. One can question the *adequacy* of those interpretations for today (a *systematic* theological question), but *historical* theology is pretty much agreed that this was the dynamic underway. Prior to the Enlightenment and the French Revolution, the last thing that the church thought was the central vocation of the Christian was to overturn the existing social order, still less to take clues on what ought to replace the old order from those formerly at the bottom of the social ladder. In my own personal opinion, the liberationist position has very important insights with which I agree, but I also believe that, in the interests of historical accuracy, the radicality and originality of these proposals should be recognized.

When one reads the Asian and African chapters of *World Religions and Human Liberation*, the commensurability question becomes more complex. Concepts such as liberation in Christianity and *mukti* (or *moksha*[12]) in

Indian traditions are similar insofar as they indicate the process of release from conditions of bondage. But they are widely divergent as they construe what constitutes that bondage. Thus, S. Painadath in *"Mukti*, the Hindu Notion of Liberation" sees the key to liberation lying in enlightenment to a state of awareness of personal estrangement, a search for release from estrangement, and a sense of the divine as mystery. Devotion, meditation, and asceticism are foundations for this release, but ultimately, liberation in Hinduism has been intepreted as coming to individuals.

Painadath is faithful to Indian tradition in depicting this liberation as an escape from an ignorance (*avidya*) of the true self (as *atman*) in an enlightenment wherein reality is revealed to be different from natural experience, which is one of blindness to the reality concealed by the appearances of the forms we encounter (*maya*). Painadath's interpretation of the *Bhagavad Gita* is intriguing; that great classic becomes a parable for mature spirituality leading one to become a warrior in pursuit of a prophetic construction of a society opposed to the caste system.

Similarly, Sulak Sivaraksa's evocative chapter, "Engaged Buddhism: Liberation from a Buddhist Perspective," shows the immense capacities of Buddhism to transpose such basic notions as *karma* from an individual to a social level. In this vein, Buddhist teaching on desire as the root of human suffering and delusion and on the proper path (*dharma*) that an enlightened individual should follow takes on new dimensions when viewed socially. And for Sivaraksa, as well as for Painadath, an Eastern religious tradition is capable of leading to a socially engaged spirituality.

The question one must raise in regard to both these contributions, however, is whether these social-ethical interpretations spring organically from the *central thrust* of Buddhist or Hindu traditions. Or are they important reinterpretations of these traditions in the light of contemporary influences and circumstances? The vector of these questions takes their direction from a seminal article by Frank Reynolds, in which he states that an adequate comparison of ethics and modes of action in two traditions needs to perform five basic operations: (1) acquire a holistic understanding of the traditions; (2) focus on their specifically ethical dimensions; (3) identify the central religio-ethical patterns; (4) investigate similarities and differences in the diverse contexts; and (5) compare how different patterns actually function in the life of the communities.[13]

Reynolds makes his specific comparison between Theravada Buddhism and Christianity, not the traditions discussed in Sivaraksa's or Painadath's chapters. But my suspicion is that Reynolds's results would not be wildly diverse if applied to the cases discussed in this book: " . . . the differences are significant, and they appear at every level."[14] At the very least, it strikes me that personal liberation from ignorance—which I use as rough shorthand for the way traditions originating in South Asia view *moksha*—is far different from changing social structures to overcome systemic evil. And this leads to a further question: For interpretations such as those of Painadath and Sivaraksa to be adopted, were modern science, dialogue with Semitic prophetic traditions, and postcolonial criticism of cultural imperialism, racism, and so forth necessary? My hunch is that without this sort of influence, a Hindu or Buddhist cultural-political and liberationist reinterpretation such as those being discussed here would not have arisen.

Discussing Josiah U. Young's "African Traditional Religion and African Theology" in the same section as that in which we examine Buddhist and Hindu notions of liberation is problematic. Still, there are rewards, chief among which is the radical nature of the commensurability problems raised by African traditional religions to the general question of liberation.

First, Young's paper is not an easy one to read. It mingles concepts and categories from African traditional religions and the contemporary blend of those traditions with elements adopted from Christianity. It is almost a truism, but a very important one, that the universe of African traditional religions are continua wherein "religion" and "ordinary" life are not radically distinguished. Most African languages, as well as most Asian languages for that matter, do not even have the concept or a word to denote it. Rather, there is "life"—and that has both visible and invisible dimensions. Young, rightly I believe, notes that such a continuum of life persists also in black African Christianity. The same can be said for black African Islam.

African Christianity is faced with three choices: beckoning from the one side is the premodern world of tradition and the vision of life in a living cosmos; beckoning from another are conservative and moderate inculturationist church leaders who see the moment as one for selecting "compatible traditional elements" for incorporation into a more or less orthodox but contextualized African Christian life; and finally, there are Young's "New Guard," attempting to draw Africans into a thoroughgoing liberationist agenda. Matters become even more complex when the aspects of traditional religion (such as divination) are incorporated into adjustment movements ("spirit churches" and "African independent churches"[15]; or into "adjustment movements" and "cargo cults" in places such as Melanesia[16]). They are undoubtedly liberationist in orientation, but often in ways very different from Latin American theological visions.

There is no doubt that in sub-Saharan Africa and parts of the world where social and historical situations are analogous (such as the islands of the Pacific), liberation themes are seed falling upon fertile ground. Young, however, does not satisfactorily answer the question of whether primal socio-religious visions would have yielded liberation theology insights without dialogue with Christian mission. Neither does Lamin Sanneh's work deal in a major way with the question of liberation motifs in traditional African cultures, but Sanneh's account of the dialogue between Christianity and African cultures does describe the interaction as one in which traditional cultures were revitalized, and out of which has grown the lively African theology discussed by Young.[17] I find it plausible to suggest that the translation process, in which dialogue occurred between Christians and Africans (the subject of Sanneh's study), was also the locus in which the need for liberation from colonial bondage—ecclesiastical, economic, and political—took the specific shape of African liberation theologies. If this is so, we again find that cross-cultural communication was midwife at the birth of latent liberation motifs.

To summarize our remarks on the commensurability of the concept of liberation in the traditions in question, the very fact that we are able to discuss the issue in some sort of logical fashion reveals a basis for comparison and, therefore, commensurability. Even so, the term "liberation theology" is not without problematics. Taking our clue from Reynolds, it seems to me that the discussion needs to take account of action-for-liberation as it emerges from religious traditions as "wholes" before the rise of our contemporary global situation. What is indubitable is that our authors show that the liberation praxis motif is capable of being subsumed into various traditions as they ponder responses to the contradictions, injustices, and outrages of the present.

That traditions as varied as those represented in this book can envisage the future as one of resisting oppression in liberationist modes, I suggest, says more about the openness of great traditions to radical reinterpretation and reorientation than it does about liberation as a central motif in their classical constitution. To that extent, liberation can fairly be called a commensurable concept. But it may have become so *as these traditions address the future more than as retrievals of their past.*[18] Finally, I observe, with Joseph Kitagawa, that it is important to say what has become a commonplace of modern political analysis also about liberative visions: that the world has many centers.[19] It is hard for me to imagine any single vision of liberation being accepted as adequate for all the world. That sort of monism leads to the stifling bureaucratization the world rejoiced to see end in Central Europe and the Soviet Union.

AMBIGUITY

In all the essays in question, there is scant mention of the possibility that the contribution of religious traditions to human liberation is *ambiguous*, rather than overwhelmingly positive. Around that question, I will organize the rest of this chapter.

Before discussing the ambiguity of such contributions, a word is required about the basic background to my thesis. It comes from an appreciation of the criticisms of religion in general, and Christianity in particular, made by five thinkers and a major modern tradition: Hume, Feuerbach, Marx, Nietzsche, and Freud, as well as the tradition of pluralistic constitutional democracies that have arisen since the eighteenth century. This is not the place to develop these criticisms at length, but it is important to realize that the figures mentioned have made many valid points on religion's *neg-*

ative impact on human development. Ignoring, for example, Nietzsche's analysis of how Christianity can lead to a posture of *ressentiment* rather than liberation seems to me simply wrong. He points to a major ambiguity in the tradition.

The lessons learned by the constitutional democracies on the importance of enforcing a relative autonomy of political, economic, cultural, and religious realms are ignored at our great risk. When any of these four dimensions of life becomes dominant, someone's rights get trampled. Liberation theologies, positively, gain their very important perspective from their origins in cultures where power is not equitably shared and perhaps even the ideals of relative autonomy exercised in democratic fashion are not observed. Their point of view on how the dominant economic structures hinder the development of the South is an important corrective to blithe cheerleading for capitalism. Negatively, though, liberation theologies run the risk of not envisaging the ambiguities of a monopolistic religious establishment becoming the leading group in social change.

To return to the mainlines of the argument. I have spoken of two basic sorts of ambiguities (one extrinsic and the other intrinsic to the way religions function). Christianity and Islam, to take the extrinsic ambiguity first, have doctrines of providence that mediate a spiritual wisdom concerning the acceptance of things that cannot be changed. But these doctrines have been utilized by ruling classes to undergird unjust political structures. This is not theory but fact. These and other religious traditions have been used to legitimate abominable practices. Secondly, even when they function at their best, the sort of conviction of "truth" and social belonging one can gain from a religious tradition can lead to fanaticism and communal strife. The creation of structures and intense feelings of social bonding are intrinsic to every religion, and thus also the possibility of that bonding being turned against others is real. Recalling the adage that the worst things are the perversion of the best, both forms of ambiguity are serious, more than merely theoretical problems.

Perhaps, you may say, reform movements can purify the tradition. Alas, another major problem swoops in when religious traditions attempt to purify themselves. They generally come from sects or special interest groups that attempt to monopolize self-understandings of the "essence" of the tradition in order to argue for their version of renewal. Reforms, though, sometimes are implemented. And then still other cliques and power blocs form to resist the reforms. Traditional hierarchies then impose order and the reformists' creativity is buried in the slow death of peacemaking by committee.

To complicate matters further, David Tracy reminds us that "classic" texts of a tradition such as Christianity are intrinsically plural. Thus apparent unity of the tradition and the utility of such texts for a progressive agenda dissolve the closer one looks at the originating sources of the tradition:

Mark's Gospel, once so clear, stable, and slightly boring ... has become in the last few years a strangely modernist document filled with interruptions, reversals, and uncanny nonendings. Luke-Acts is still received in conflicting ways by very different Christian groups: charismatics appealing to the role of the Spirit in these texts, liberation and political theologians insisting upon the preferential option for the poor, liberal Christians content with Luke's rather common-sensical account of Jesus, Barthians anxious to show how Luke resembles a nineteenth-century realistic novel's rendering the true identity of the main character through its historylike narrative.[20]

For Tracy, the hermeneutical problem lies in the fact that every classic (1) has elements that lend themselves to a stable interpretation around which life can be organized (for example, the Lucan common life ideal in Acts 4:32 when used as inspiration for maintaining a simple life in community); but also (2) exhibits a "surplus of meaning" that becomes the breeding ground for ever new interpretations as diverse places and times call forth new interpretations (for example, Luke 4:18's retrieval of Isaiah 61:1–2 when used by Christian base communities to justify an activist stance against a corrupt social order that may include the hierarchy's own version of a faithful community).

If Tracy is right, what becomes of the Christian tradition "as a whole"? The short answer is that it becomes slippery in the extreme, and attempts to enforce solutions to problems often end up in terrible acts of ecclesiastical repression. I have heard, for example, many compare Vatican attempts to effect "unity of faith" with those of the Kremlin. Khomeini's Iran is also a possible example. And the state of Israel wraps itself in the mantle of Judaism when many otherwise sensitive persons suspect power politics is at play. And the examples are not always simple: when Elisabeth Schüssler Fiorenza reconstructs Christian origins and finds a repressed subversive tradition of Jesus as a woman-identified man, what becomes of the Vatican's construal of the "apostolic tradition" as barring women from ordained ministry?[21] If a candidate for the Catholic episcopacy were to accept Schüssler Fiorenza's reconstructions of Christian origins, he would be barred from assuming a higher leadership role in the church, in effect ruling out an honest debate on the matter.[22]

Schüssler Fiorenza gives a reading on an important aspect of interest to Christianity as a whole; but so does the Congregation for the Doctrine of the Faith. It is also clear that these two construals of Christianity, though incompatible, both rest on firm documentary evidence. Coming to an agreement seems impossible, and only a political victory can vindicate one or the other side. Thus do inner plurality and radical ambiguity reveal themselves in a church that takes human liberation to be an integral part of sharing the gospel.

The reason for raising this intra-Christian dispute is to heighten aware-

ness that Christian tradition is ambiguous as a resource for women's liberation, and they are half of humankind. Moreover, it seems that there was
a coverup of Jesus' rather more freeing attitudes toward women during his
ministry, and this throws into confusion some of the tradition's most hal-
lowed notions of earliest Christianity. Now this may not disturb those who
believe Christianity is basically about the retrieval of the historical Jesus,
for in Schüssler Fiorenza's reconstructions they believe that they are recovering the essence of Christianity in getting closer to the history of Jesus.
But if one examines the New Testament *as a whole*, one finds Christianity
has never been merely "about Jesus." Rather, it has exemplified a dynamic
wherein the presence of the Spirit and God (*ho theos*) are as integral as
was the Jesus of history, as is made especially clear in the dynamic portrayed
in Luke-Acts.[23] What are we to do with the inference that the very redactors
of the narratives that formed the Scriptures seem to have been in league
with apostolic church leaders (the "apostles" and their "successors," if I
may use shorthand for a very complicated theological construction) to distort the history of Jesus? These leaders, after all, are the ones whom the
church believes were specially guided in establishing the primitive community.

A particularly graphic statement on the source of multiple valid interpretations of the Christian essence is found in the words of Paul Johnson,
which I wish to make my own. He observes that the teaching of Jesus, as
best we can grasp it, is

> more a series of glimpses, or matrices, a collection of insights, rather
> than a code of doctrine. It invites comment, interpretation, elabora-
> tion and constructive argument, and it is the starting point for rival,
> though compatible, lines of inquiry. It is not a summa theologica, or
> indeed ethica, but the basis from which an endless series of summae
> can be assembled. It inaugurates a religion of dialogue, exploration
> and experiment. Its radical elements are balanced by conservative
> qualifications, there is a constant mixture of legalism and antinomi-
> anism, and the emphasis repeatedly switches from rigor and militancy
> to acquiescence and the acceptance of suffering. Some of this variety
> reflects the genuine bewilderment of the disciples and the confusion
> of the evangelical editors to whom their memories descended. But a
> great deal is essentially part of Jesus' universalist posture: the wonder
> is that the personality behind the mission is in no way fragmented but
> is always integrated and true to character. Jesus contrives to be all
> things to all men while remaining faithful to himself.[24]

A prime source of ambiguity in every religious tradition may lie in the
fact that in any succession of historical periods, the dynamics that traditions
unleash call forth now one and now another dialectically related response.
The origins of basic concretizations of religious ideals lie in such conflicts,

and it is not clear that their solution is unidirectionally linear toward a better situation. Religious traditions, I maintain, can never be finally finished because of their process nature as socio-cultural-religious syntheses. The goal of settling down, in fact, is an illusion, and this may nowhere be truer than in attempts to return always to the history of Jesus to settle issues, rather than by doing christological reflection on the journey into the future.[25]

In an age when history moved slowly, the contradictions between, for example, the side of Jesus and apostolic church life that accentuated continuity, love, and stability, on the one hand (Acts 4:32), and the side that gave warrants for radical change, prophetic judgment, and revolution, on the other hand (Luke 4:18), were not so evident. The contradictions can, for instance, be papered over in the way Elisabeth Schüssler Fiorenza shows they were in concealing the identification of Jesus with sophia-God and women! We live in a world where burying such conflicts is increasingly difficult. Thus centers of religiously justified stability bequeathed to society by one concretization of a religious ideal (for example, the caste system or an ordered family life with males at the head) become a rival interpretation's abomination (for example, Gandhi's or the feminists').

The problem of internal "plurality" and ambiguity in religious traditions, when viewed in the light of the demands of liberative praxis, is immense. To which Judaism are we to appeal for light on transforming the future? That of David Ben Gurion, Moses, Abraham Heschel, Maimonides? Which Catholicism? Which Buddhism? Which African tradition? Which Confucianism?

While I find reassuring the words of Cohn-Sherbok, Ally, Painadath, Sivaraksa, and Young on the appropriation of liberation ideals in their respective traditions, the question remains: Is the legacy of these traditions as ambiguous and plural as the Christian? An affirmative answer makes advisable: (1) profound reservations on the liberative potential of any religious tradition; (2) a modest view of the role of religion in effecting human liberation; and (3) a positive response to the liberal democratic traditions' insistence that religion, politics, economics, and the arts be relatively autonomous, lest one interest group impose its will by force on any or all the others, as happened in the Leninist-Stalinist hegemony where one group's political interests dominated over all others in Russia.

As a Christian whose direct knowledge of a radically "other" tradition is confined to time spent in Melanesia, I hesitate to do more than suggest the possibility of a problem in other religions. My hunch, though is that their problems are at least as deep as those of the Christian (post-Christian?) North.

We live in a world where what happens in one tradition has an impact on others. Indeed, John B. Cobb, Jr., has argued that our paradigm for interreligious relations should be one of moving beyond "dialogue" to "mutual transformation."[26] This idea of Cobb's has influenced my own personal view of how things will and probably should move. Painadath's and Sulak Sivaraksa's contributions to this book are certainly proof that Western traditions could profit mightily from Eastern.

A sage observation by Sharon Welch should make us cautious about the prognosis for radical social transformation and whether liberation theology as we presently know it has the answer to our problems:

> [The] type of humanity envisioned by liberation theologians does not come about naturally; it has to be achieved. This type of human community is not a given; it must be fought for. Even then, it can be, and often is, destroyed in history. It is to be achieved, not merely recognized. Liberation theology is part of a struggle for the establishment of a particular kind of subjectivity, not a declaration of the a priori existence of that subjectivity.[27]

Much romantic discussion about liberation, I fear, ignores Whitehead's cautions about the fallacy of "misplaced concreteness": imagining that a concrete reality (that is, a liberative agency) corresponds to an abstraction (liberative ideals).[28] Welch's remarks are a healthy antidote to that fallacy. Liberation is not a matter of fruitful ideas, even though correct ideas are helpful. Rather, as Welch states it so well, real people need to be formed in actual communities to do the concrete work of social transformation.

In similar fashion, the challenge of *World Religions and Human Liberation* lies not in whether one can find elements in the several traditions analogous to liberation theology motifs. For each of the world's great traditions has in it elements that can contribute fruitfully to understanding human liberation as we together confront our tragic age. The more vital issue is fourfold. First, will the ambiguities of these traditions act as a brake to the process of emancipatory action? Second, where will be formed the concrete communities needed to nurture Welch's new kind of subjects? Third, as members of the various traditions face the future, will the sort of association they form lead to a common effort to liberate humanity? Fourth, will that common effort lead to a new kind of cross-tradition pollination and eventually to an entirely new incorporation of diverse genetic strands in the search for human liberty and unity?

NOTES

1. Paul Tillich, in *Systematic Theology*, 3 vols. (Chicago: University of Chicago Press, 1951–63), 3:98. See the entire section, pp. 92–110, for a fuller development of the idea including where Tillich goes so far as to consider religion as "demonic."

2. Paul F. Knitter, "Toward a Liberation Theology of Religions," in John Hick and Paul F. Knitter, eds., *The Myth of Christian Uniqueness: Toward a Pluralistic Theology of Religions* (Maryknoll, N.Y.: Orbis Books, 1987), pp. 178–200.

3. Joseph M. Kitagawa, *Spiritual Liberation and Human Freedom in Contem-*

porary Asia (New York: Peter Lang, 1990), p. 125 (emphasis added).

4. See David Bosch, *Transforming Mission: Paradigm Shifts in Theology of Mission* (Maryknoll, N.Y.: Orbis Books, 1991), pp. 498–504.

5. Gustavo Gutiérrez, trans. Matthew J. O'Connell, *The Truth Shall Make You Free* (Maryknoll, N.Y.: Orbis Books, 1990), pp. 3–4.

6. Ibid., pp. 142–43.

7. See, for example, Seyyed Hossein Nasr, *Islam and the Plight of Modern Man* (New York: Longman), pp. 130–48.

8. See St. Bonaventure, *Breviloquium*, II:5 (Paterson, N.J.: St. Anthony Press, 1963), pp. 81–87.

9. Ernst Troeltsch, in *The Social Teaching of the Christian Churches*, trans. Olive Wyon, 2 vols. (Chicago: University of Chicago Press, 1976), 1:246–51 and *passim*, sees this attempt to make the temporal world reflect the eternal as a key to understanding medieval social ethics as a concretization of the original love ethic of Jesus.

10. Important for me have been insights from Richard J. Cassidy, *Society and Politics in the Acts of the Apostles* (Maryknoll, N.Y.: Orbis Books, 1987); Abraham J. Malherbe, *Social Aspects of Early Christianity*, 2nd ed., (Philadelphia: Fortress, 1983); Wayne A. Meeks, *The First Urban Christians: The Social World of the Apostle Paul* (New Haven: Yale University Press, 1983); and John Howard Yoder, *The Politics of Jesus* (Grand Rapids, Mich.: Eerdmans, 1972).

11. See Bernard J. F. Lonergan, trans. Conn O'Donovan, *The Way to Nicea: The Dialectical Development of Trinitarian Theology* (Philadelphia: Westminster, 1976); and Jaroslav Pelikan, *The Christian Tradition*, vol. 1: *The Emergence of the Catholic Tradition* (100-600) (Chicago: University of Chicago Press, 1971), pp. 121–71; 226–77.

12. Painadath uses *mukti* instead of the more common *moksha* throughout his essay. The roots of both words lie in the Sanskrit *muc*. *Mukti*, I am informed by my Indologist friend, David Carpenter of St. Joseph University, Philadelphia, has the sense of an activity and is a verbal noun; *moksha* has the flavor of the result of that release.

13. Frank Reynolds, "Contrasting Modes of Action: A Comparative Study of Buddhist and Christian Ethics," *History of Religions* 20 (August/November 1980): 130–31.

14. Ibid., p. 136.

15. See M.L. Daneel, *The Quest for Belonging* (Harare: Mambo Press, 1987). An excellent collection edited by Edward Fashole-Luke et al., *Christianity in Independent Africa* (Bloomington, Ind.: Indiana University Press, 1978), though aging, discusses African Christianity and theology from every conceivable side.

16. See Kenelm Burridge, *New Heaven New Earth: A Study of Millenarian Activities* (New York: Schocken, 1969); *Mambu: A Melanesian Millennium* (London: Methuen & Co., 1960).

17. See Lamin Sanneh, *Translating the Message: The Missionary Impact on Culture* (Maryknoll, N.Y.: Orbis Books, 1989), pp. 182–90.

18. Joseph M. Kitagawa's *Spiritual Liberation and Human Freedom in Contemporary Asia*, op. cit., is an excellent historical approach to these dynamics. His use of Augustine's *Confessions*, XVIII, 52 in the former (pp. 178–79) is especially suggestive in reminding us of three sorts of historical presence: (1) the present of things past; (2) the present of things present; and (3) the present of things future. I hope I do not stretch Kitagawa's point unduly when I suggest that, in the case of

142   William R. Burrows

the liberation ideal, the many traditions today increasingly include each others' pasts, modify them, and image the future differently than they would have without the juxtaposition of "religious-cultural-social-political" syntheses Kitagawa discusses in *The Quest for Human Unity: A Religious History* (Minneapolis: Fortress, 1990).

19. Kitagawa, *Spiritual Liberation*, pp. 136ff.

20. David Tracy, *Plurality and Ambiguity: Hermeneutics, Religion, Hope* (San Francisco: Harper & Row, 1987), pp. 13–14.

21. Compare the interpretation of Christian fellowship in Elisabeth Schüssler Fiorenza, *In Memory of Her: A Feminist Theological Reconstruction of Christian Origins* (New York: Crossroad, 1983), pp. 130–54 with that found in Congregation for the Doctrine of the Faith, "Delcaratio circa Quaestionem Admissionis Mulierum ad Sacerdotium Ministeriale," *Acta Apostolicae Sedis* 69 (1977): 98–116.

22. See Michael H. Crosby, *The Dysfunctional Church: Addiction and Codependence in the Family of Catholicism* (Notre Dame, Ind.: Ave Maria Press, 1991). Crosby argues that the refusal to debate such issues seriously creates systemic perversions in the Roman Catholic church.

23. See Norman Perrin, *The New Testament: An Introduction* (New York: Harcourt Brace Jovanovich, 1974), pp. 195–205; Ernst Haenchen, *The Acts of the Apostles*, trans. R. Wilson (Philadelphia: Westminster, 1971); and David M. Stanley, *The Apostolic Church in the New Testament* (Westminister, Maryland: Newman, 1965), pp. 5–37.

24. Paul Johnson, *A History of Christianity* (New York: Atheneum, 1980), p. 28.

25. I owe this family of insights especially to process thought, more concretely to John B. Cobb, Jr., whose *Christ in a Pluralistic Age* (Philadelphia: Westminster, 1975) remains for me a profoundly suggestive meditation on the relationship between concrete origins of Christianity in Jesus and the dynamic processes of history.

26. See John B. Cobb, Jr., *Beyond Dialogue: Toward a Mutual Transformation of Christianity and Buddhism* (Philadelphia: Fortress, 1982), pp. 47–53, 140.

27. Sharon D. Welch, *Communities of Resistance and Solidarity: A Feminist Theology of Liberation* (Maryknoll, N.Y.: Orbis Books, 1985), p. 66.

28. Alfred North Whitehead, *Science in the Modern World* (New York: Macmillan, 1925), pp. 51–55.